FINANCIAL SECTOR OF THE AMERICAN ECONOMY

T0347956

edited by

STUART BRUCHEY
ALLAN NEVINS PROFESSOR EMERITUS
COLUMBIA UNIVERSITY

PRICING OPTIONS WITH FUTURES-STYLE MARGINING

A Genetic Adaptive Neural Network Approach

A. JAY WHITE

Routledge
Taylor & Francis Group

LONDON AND NEW YORK

First published 2000 by Garland Publishing Inc.

2 Park Square, Milton Park, Abingdon, Oxon OX14 4RN
711 Third Avenue, New York, NY 10017, USA

Routledge is an imprint of the Taylor & Francis Group, an informa business

First issued in paperback 2016

Library of Congress Cataloging-in-Publication Data

White, A. Jay.
  Pricing options with futures-style margining : a genetic adaptive neural network approach / A. Jay White.
      p. cm. — (Financial sector of the American economy)
    Includes bibliographical references and index.
    ISBN 0-8153-3392-7 (alk. paper)
    1. Options (Finance)—Prices—Mathematical models. 2. Futures—Mathematical models. 3. Neural networks. I. Title. II. Series.
  HG6024.A3 W8 1999
  332.64'5 21—dc21   99-041196

ISBN 978-0-8153-3392-0 (hbk)
ISBN 978-1-138-98668-8 (pbk)

To Susan, A.J., and Dori

Contents

Tables

Figures

Acknowledgments

Numerous individuals have played a part in the completion of this book. I would like to thank my Ph.D. chair at the University of Mississippi, Dr. Gay B. Hatfield, for her guidance, patience, and encouragement. Her support and advice has benefited me both personally and professionally over the years that I have known her. Her advice was the catalyst that led me to pursue my doctorate. I would also like to thank Dr. Robert Dorsey, and Dr. Colby Kullman, also of the University of Mississippi, whose expertise and suggestions were critical for the completion of this project. Credit is certainly also due to the numerous participants at the 1998 Midwest Finance Association meeting and 1997 Southern and Southwest Finance Association meetings whose comments and suggestions on some of my research projects found their way into this book.

Last but certainly not least, I would like to thank my wife, Susan, for her encouragement, understanding and sacrifice throughout this endeavor. Without her support, it is unlikely that I would have seen this project through fruition.

Pricing Options with Futures-Style Margining

CHAPTER I

Introduction

In 1973, options on stock became available on an organized exchange when the Chicago Board of Trade created the Chicago Board Options Exchange (CBOE). Options existed prior to this time, but the contracts lacked standardization and a central exchange. Since that introduction, the options market has experienced tremendous growth and has spawned even more exotic types of derivative securities. Besides the CBOE, options are now traded on numerous exchanges worldwide, including: the Philadelphia Stock Exchange (PHLX), the American Stock Exchange (AMEX), the New York Stock Exchange (NYSE), the Chicago Mercantile Exchange (CME), the London International Financial Futures and Options Exchange (LIFFE), and many others.

Though the exchanges on which options are traded are numerous, the types of options that are available are even more numerous. Options contracts are available on stocks, stock indexes, debt instruments, Treasury securities, interest rates, currencies, and on futures contracts, which can themselves be based on numerous underlying assets. Most of these futures options tend to be based on financial assets such as options on interest rate futures or stock index futures.

An option is a contract that gives the owner the right, but not the obligation, to do something. A call option gives the buyer the right, but not the obligation, to buy the underlying asset at a pre-specified price within a certain period of time. A put option gives the buyer the right to sell the underlying asset at a pre-specified price within a certain period of time. If the option can only be exercised at the option's expiration date, it is a European style option. If the option can be exercised at any time prior to expiration, it is an American style option. For example, a call option on the Japanese Yen might give the buyer the right to purchase ¥6,250,000 at .0097$/¥ (for a total of $60,625) on or before March 10, 1995 if American-style. If the call is European-style, it may be exercised only on March 10, 1995.

With a traditional options contract, the buyer pays the seller an amount called a premium, and the option seller must post margin. The buyer pays the full amount of the premium, and unless the option is exercised, there are no further payment requirements. This premium is used by the seller of the option to post margin. It is possible that the option seller will have to post additional funds if the option's value increases. This is similar to the short investor's position in a typical futures contract. For the option buyer to realize any gain, however, the option must be exercised or sold. In some cases (currency or cross-rate options), the margin requirement for the option writer can be satisfied with a letter of credit from an approved bank.

An alternate method of handling these contracts is to have both the buyer and seller post margin and then require marking to market as with futures contracts. With this type of system, the option buyer (long position) and the option seller (short position) would deposit funds (initial margin) in a margin account. At the end of each trading day, the option value would be marked to market, and the margin account would be adjusted to show the investor's gain or loss. If there is an increase in the option's price, the short investor's margin account would be reduced while the long investor's margin account would be increased. The reverse would occur if there is a decrease in the option's price. With this system the long position (option buyer) still has the right to exercise the option.

Currently, futures-style options are traded on the London International Financial Futures and Options Exchange (LIFFE) and on the Sydney Futures Exchange, but not on exchanges in the United States. Although not yet approved, it had been proposed by the CME and the Chicago Board of Trade to switch to a futures-style margining system for options on futures contracts. According to Lieu (1990), The Chicago Futures Trading Commission (CFTC) had several concerns about such a change. These concerns included the fact that a change to futures-style margining could lead to differences in option prices. The reasoning by the CFTC was that short investors would require a larger premium to compensate for interest lost on full premiums and that longs would be willing to pay a higher price because they would be gaining that interest income. At the time of this writing, the CME has yet to adopt a futures-style margining system for any of its contracts.

To date, few researchers have addressed the pricing of options with futures-style margining. Lieu (1990) derived a new option pricing model to price futures-style options (futures options). By noting that a futures-style option is effectively a futures contract on an option, Lieu uses the same arbitrage-free principles as did Black & Scholes (1973). However, because interest rate futures contracts do not satisfy the distributional assumptions that are part of the Black-Scholes type models, Lieu states his model cannot be used to price futures-style options on interest rate futures.

Chen & Scott (1993) show that Lieu's results apply in a general equilibrium setting with stochastic interest rates and therefore can be applied to futures-style options on interest rate futures. These authors then go on to show how interest rate futures options can be priced under various interest rate models. All of the models derived depend on the assumption of a continuous process for the underlying asset. Furthermore, the models ignore the impact of marking-to-market on traders' cash flows and are applicable only for futures-style options on non-coupon bearing securities.

Although a great deal of work has been done in the area of option pricing, there still exists a number of problems related to estimating or predicting option prices. Some of these problems include but are not limited to:

1. There are no closed-form solutions to most American-style options. They must be approximated with some analytical methodology which usually requires the stipulation of a number of assumptions and the estimation of supporting parameters.

2. Most option pricing models are based on the assumption that the underlying security follows some stochastic process. In reality, there is no way of knowing what the true process is which determines the underlying security's price path.

3. With the exception of some interest rate derivative pricing models, most option pricing models assume that the risk-free rate is constant. The models that do allow the risk-free rate to vary are bound by some specification as to how interest rates are determined.

4. Most option pricing models specify that the underlying
    security's volatility is fixed. Research [Hull and White (1987),
    Johnson and Shannon (1987), Scott (1987), and Wiggins
    (1987)] has shown that if volatilities are stochastic, then Black-
    Scholes type models produce pricing biases. If we assume
    stochastic volatility, we must assume some underlying
    distribution for the volatility. Furthermore, if we assume
    stochastic volatility, no explicit solutions for option prices exist
    and prices must be estimated using numerical methods.

5. Pricing biases exist in many of the existing option pricing
    models indicating the possibility that certain macroeconomic
    variables which affect option prices are being omitted in option
    pricing analysis. These biases also may indicate that the
    assumptions as to the distribution of the underlying security's
    value may be misspecified.

6. Many "special" types of options do not have models available
    that fully take into account their characteristics (for example,
    this study will focus on options with futures style margining).
    Although extensions of basic models have been developed to
    price these types of options, none of the extension models take
    into account the impact of marking-to-market on traders' cash
    flows. Secondly, these models are applicable only for futures-
    style options on non-coupon bearing securities. While this
    second short-coming is not a problem for options on T-bills,
    Eurodollars, and other non-coupon bearing securities, it does
    limit the scope of such models.

Although many different types of option pricing models have been
developed to try to address some of the above problems, none of the
approximation techniques developed apply uniformly to the many
different types of options.

RESEARCH OBJECTIVE

The purpose of this study is to utilize Genetic Adaptive Neural
Networks (GANNs) to develop a method of pricing futures options
with futures-style margining. The primary goals of this study will be to:

1. Establish the GANNs ability to approximate a pre-specified option pricing function through simulation.

2. Develop an artificial neural network that will accurately price futures options with futures-style margining using real data.

3. Examine the effects of incorporating additional economic data into the pricing of futures options when using GANNs.

As secondary objectives, this study will compare the GANNs ability to price futures options with futures-style margining with current option pricing approximation techniques.

SCOPE AND LIMITATIONS

In order to address the first goal, this study will simulate call and put option prices using an alternative option pricing model and arbitrary parameters. This data will be presented to the GANN to determine the GANN's ability to approximate the function used to derive the simulated data.

To address the second goal, the GANN will then be presented with real data provided by the London International Financial Futures and Options Exchange (LIFFE) to determine the GANN's ability to accurately price futures options with futures-style margining. The specific option contract that will be examined will be the Eurodollar (ED) futures option. The period examined will be January 1994 to July 1994.

Once the GANN has been presented with the real data, a holdout sample will be presented to determine the GANNs ability to accurately price these options. The GANNs option pricing predictions will be compared to a derivation of Black's (1976) option pricing model as a benchmark.

ORGANIZATION

Chapter II provides a review of the literature relevant to option pricing. The first section reviews the seminal Black-Scholes (1973) analysis of stock option pricing and some extensions of this basic model. The second section reviews the Binomial Option Pricing Model (BOPM) and analytical models developed to compensate for some of the shortcomings of the basic B-S model. Literature related to "special" options such as options on currency, options on indices, and options on futures (futures options) is covered in the third section while interest rate derivative securities (options on interest bearing securities) are discussed in the fourth section. The literature concerning options with futures style margining is discussed in the fifth section. The sixth section covers some empirical studies on option pricing models, and the chapter is concluded with a brief summary of the reviewed literature.

The methodology and sample will be presented in Chapter III. The simulation data set is discussed in the first section, while the second and third sections cover the real data set and the neural network methodology, respectively. A discussion of previous neural network applications for finance, including option valuation and hedging, can be found in the section on neural network methodology.

The results of this study are given in Chapter IV. The GANNs ability to approximate an underlying and unknown option pricing function will be presented in the first section. The second section will present the results of applying the ANN to real data. The results of the ANNs comparison to the adjusted Black's (1976) model (denoted BS_{CS} OPM) in predicting option prices will also be presented in this section. In the third section, the results of incorporating additional economic data with the ANNs will be examined. The conclusions will be presented in the final chapter, Chapter V. Suggestions for future research will also be provided in this chapter.

CHAPTER II

Literature Review

This chapter introduces and reviews the literature relating to modern option pricing theory. There are six sections in this chapter, each dealing with a different aspect of contingency security pricing. The first section reviews the seminal Black-Scholes (1973) analysis of stock option pricing and some extensions of this basic model. The second section reviews the Binomial Option Pricing Model (BOPM) and analytical models developed to compensate for some of the shortcomings of the basic B-S model. Literature related to "special" options such as options on currency, options on indices, and options on futures (futures options) is covered in the third section while interest rate derivative securities are discussed in the fourth section. The literature concerning options with futures style margining is discussed in the fifth section. This is a relatively new area for options research which has received little attention. Finally, the sixth section covers some empirical studies on option pricing models, and the chapter is then concluded with a brief summary of the reviewed literature.

SECTION I: BLACK-SCHOLES AND EXTENSIONS

Many of the option pricing models used today are an extension of or were derived in a manner similar to that of the model developed by Fischer Black and Myron Scholes (1973). It is therefore appropriate to conduct a somewhat detailed review of the Black-Scholes (B-S) model.

Black-Scholes

Black-Scholes (1973) developed the first closed-form solution to option pricing. Their model priced European call options and was devised by forming a riskless portfolio consisting of a position in a non-dividend paying stock and a position in a derivative security (a call option) on that stock. B-S noted both the stock price and the derivative security price are affected by the same source of uncertainty. This implies that the stock and the derivative security are perfectly positively correlated (for a call option) for a short period of time. If one has two assets that are perfectly correlated, a riskless portfolio can be created by buying one of the assets and selling (shorting) the other. With such a portfolio, a gain in one of the assets will be exactly offset by a loss on the other asset such that the portfolio value is unchanged. Black-Scholes next set the return on this riskless portfolio equal to the risk-free rate of interest. Black-Scholes make the following assumptions when deriving their formula:

1. The short-term interest rate is known and is constant through time.

2. The stock price follows a random walk in continuous time with a variance rate proportional to the square of the stock price. This implies that the distribution of possible stock prices at the end of any finite interval is log-normal. The variance rate of return on the stock is constant. More specifically, the price of the underlying stock follows a process described by:

$$dS = \mu S dt + \sigma S dw \qquad (2.1)$$

where:

S = initial stock price.
μ = the instantaneous expected rate of return on stock.
σ = the instantaneous standard deviation of the rate of return.
dw = a standard Wiener process[1].
dt = some small increment of time.

3. The stock pays no dividends or other distributions.
4. The option is European style (can only be exercised at maturity).

5. There are no transaction costs in buying or selling the stock or the option.

6. It is possible to borrow any fraction of the price of a security to buy it or to hold it, at the short-term interest rate.

7. There are no infringements upon short selling.

Black-Scholes state that "under these assumptions, the value of the option will depend only on the price of the stock and time and on variables that are taken to be known constants."

If we assume that the stock price S follows the process outlined in Equation 2.1 above, and let c be the price of a call option on S, then Ito's lemma[2] can be applied to Equation 2.1 to give:

$$dc = \left(\frac{\partial c}{\partial S} \mu S + \frac{\partial c}{\partial t} + \frac{1}{2} \frac{\partial^2 c}{\partial S^2} \sigma^2 S^2 \right) dt + \frac{\partial c}{\partial S} \sigma S dw \qquad (2.2)$$

Both Equation 2.1 and 2.2 can be written in discrete time as:

$$\Delta S = \mu S \Delta t + \sigma S \Delta w \qquad (2.3)$$

and

$$\Delta c = \left(\frac{\partial c}{\partial S} \mu S + \frac{\partial c}{\partial t} + \frac{1}{2} \frac{\partial^2 c}{\partial S^2} \sigma^2 S^2 \right) \Delta t + \frac{\partial c}{\partial S} \sigma S \Delta w \qquad (2.4)$$

where Δc and ΔS are the changes in c and S for some small change in time Δt. In equation 2.2, both c and S are affected by the same Wiener process dw. This means that when we form our risk-less portfolio that consists of buying one asset and shorting the other, we can eliminate the Wiener process. The value of our hedge portfolio, P_H, will be equal to the sum of the value of the two securities that make up the portfolio, $P_H = -c + hS$ (we sell one call option and buy h shares of the stock at price S). Therefore:

$$\Delta P_H = -\Delta c + h \Delta S \qquad (2.5)$$

and substituting Equations 2.3 and 2.4 into 2.5 gives:

$$\Delta P_H = -\left(\frac{\partial c}{\partial t} \mu S + \frac{\partial c}{\partial t} + \frac{1}{2} \frac{\partial^2 c}{\partial S^2} \sigma^2 S^2 \right) \Delta t + \left(h - \frac{\partial c}{\partial S} \right) \sigma S \Delta w + h \mu S \Delta t \qquad (2.6)$$

If c and S are both affected by the same uncertainty, Δw, then in order to completely eliminate risk, we must purchase $h = \partial c / \partial S$ shares of the stock. Doing so allows the Wiener process to drop out of the equation and, after simplifying, we are left with:

$$\Delta P_H = -\left(\frac{\partial c}{\partial t} + \frac{1}{2}\frac{\partial^2 c}{\partial S^2}\sigma^2 S^2\right)\Delta t \tag{2.7}$$

which is riskless over time Δt. In order to preclude arbitrage, this riskless portfolio must earn the same return as other risk-less assets in the market, therefore, this portfolio must earn the risk-free rate, r. This implies that $\Delta P_H = rP_H\Delta t$, and substituting for P_H and ΔP_H gives:

$$-\left(\frac{\partial c}{\partial t} + \frac{1}{2}\frac{\partial^2 c}{\partial S^2}\sigma^2 S^2\right)\Delta t = r\left(-c + \frac{\partial c}{\partial S}\right)\Delta t \tag{2.8}$$

simplifying:

$$\frac{\partial c}{\partial t} + rS\frac{\partial c}{\partial S} + \frac{1}{2}\frac{\partial^2 c}{\partial S^2}\sigma^2 S^2 = rc \tag{2.9}$$

Equation 2.9 is basically the same differential equation derived by Black-Scholes. This differential equation is non-stochastic, as the only stochastic term, dS, has dropped out of the equation. If f is defined as any derivative security on S and c is replaced with f in equation 2.9 above, the result is a general arbitrage equation for valuing derivative securities. The equation has infinite solutions, and the solution will depend on the boundary conditions of the derivative security. In this case, a call option that can only be exercised at expiration, time = T, is being valued. The boundary conditions for a European style call option are:

$$c = \max(S_T - X, 0) \text{ at time } t = T, \tag{2.10}$$

where S_T is the stock price at time T and X is the option's exercise price. If $S_T > X$, the value of the option is $S_T - X$, otherwise the value of the option is 0.

The solution to Equation 2.9 can be found by transforming that equation into the heat exchange equation used in physics. According to Smith (1990), a more intuitive approach would be to simplify the structure by assuming the simplest form of risk-preference, risk-neutrality. Most investors are considered risk-adverse, meaning they require a premium above the risk-free rate, r, in order to induce them to invest in a risky security. A risk-neutral investor requires no such premium, and in a risk-neutral world, the expected return on all assets is the risk-free rate. Notice that in Equation (2.9) the term μ (the expected return on the stock) has dropped out of the equation. If μ had remained, the use of risk-neutrality would not have been possible as for higher levels of risk, and investors would demand a larger risk premium which would lead to a larger μ. Because μ drops out, however, life is simplified, and the assumption of risk-neutrality can be retained.

As stated above, in a risk neutral world, the expected rate of return on all assets would be the same and that rate would be the risk-free rate. This implies that the value of the call today (time t) is the present value of the expected terminal value, discounted at the risk-free rate:

$$c = e^{-r(T-t)} E\left[\max(S_T - X, 0)\right].$$ (2.11)

If S_T is lognormally distributed, then 2.11 can be re-written as:

$$c = e^{-r(T-t)} \int_{X}^{\infty} (S_T - X) L'(S_T) dS_T,$$ (2.12)

where $L''(S_T)$ is the log normally distributed density function. Following Smith (1990), the solution to such a problem can be found using the following theorem

Theorem. If is a log-normally distributed density function with

$$V = \begin{cases} 0, & \text{if } S_T > \gamma X \\ \phi S_T - \lambda X, & \text{if } \gamma X \geq S_T \geq \theta X \\ 0, & \text{if } S_T < \theta X. \end{cases}$$

Then

$$E[V] = \int_{\theta X}^{\gamma X} (\phi S_T - \lambda X) L(S_T) dS_T$$

$$e^{\rho(T-t)}\phi S\left[\left\{\frac{\ln\left(\frac{S}{\theta X}\right)+\left(\rho+\frac{\sigma^2}{2}\right)(T-t)}{\sigma\sqrt{T-t}}\right\}-N\left\{\frac{\ln\left(\frac{S}{\gamma X}\right)+\left(\rho+\frac{\sigma^2}{2}\right)(T-t)}{\sigma\sqrt{T-t}}\right\}\right]$$

$$-\lambda X\left[N\left\{\frac{\ln\left(\frac{S}{\theta X}\right)+\left(\rho-\frac{\sigma^2}{2}\right)(T-t)}{\sigma\sqrt{T-t}}\right\}-N\left\{\frac{\ln\left(\frac{S}{\gamma X}\right)+\left(\rho+\frac{\sigma^2}{2}\right)(T-t)}{\sigma\sqrt{T-t}}\right\}\right]$$

where θ, γ, ϕ, and λ are arbitrary parameters and ρ is the average expected rate of growth in

$$S\left(\textit{E}\left[S_T/S\right]\right)=e^{\rho(T-t)}$$

and $N\{\cdot\}$ is the cumulative probability distribution for a standardized normal variable. Because we are assuming risk-neutrality, $\rho=r$ and by setting $\phi=\lambda=e^{-r(T-t)}$, $\theta=1$, and $\gamma=\infty$ we can solve 2.12 by applying the above substitutions into theorem 1. The solution is

$$c=SN(d_1)-Xe^{-r(T-t)}N(d_2) \tag{2.13}$$

where

$$d_1=\frac{\ln\left(\frac{S}{X}\right)+\left(r+\frac{\sigma^2}{2}\right)(T-t)}{\sigma\sqrt{T-t}} \quad \text{and} \tag{2.13a}$$

$$d_2=\frac{\ln\left(\frac{S}{X}\right)+\left(r-\frac{\sigma^2}{2}\right)(T-t)}{\sigma\sqrt{T-t}}=d_1-\sigma\sqrt{T-t}. \tag{2.13b}$$

The inputs for 2.13 are the current stock price, S, the option's exercise price, X, the stock price's variance, σ^2, time to maturity, $T - t$, and the risk-free rate of interest, r. If we define $T - t$ as τ, 2.13 can be expressed as

$$c = c\left(S, X, r, \sigma^2, \tau\right), \tag{2.14}$$

and the partial effects are

$$\frac{\partial c}{\partial S} > 0; \quad \frac{\partial c}{\partial \sigma^2} > 0; \quad \frac{\partial c}{\partial X} < 0; \quad \frac{\partial c}{\partial r} > 0; \quad \frac{\partial c}{\partial \tau} > 0.$$

These partials indicate a direct relationship between the stock price and the value of a call. As the value of the stock increases, the value of the call option must also increase, other things equal. There is an indirect relationship between the exercise price, X, and the value of the call. A large exercise price means that the stock price must rise significantly to be in-the-money. Therefore, a large exercise price corresponds to a small call value. There is a direct relationship between the price of the call and the stock's volatility, σ^2. The stock's price has a lower bound of 0, but there is no upper bound; so with a larger volatility, the probability of a higher stock price is greater and so is the value of the call. The same argument holds for the time to maturity. When τ is large, there is a greater probability of a larger stock price and, therefore, a larger call price. Also, if τ is large, the exercise price is being discounted over a longer period which translates into a small present value for the exercise price and a larger value for the call. There is also a direct relationship between the value of a call and the risk-free rate. Discounting the value of the exercise at a large risk-free rate translates into a smaller present value for the exercise price. This in turn translates into a larger call value.

Although a similar analysis can be used to value a European put option that doesn't pay dividends, it is easier to apply put-call parity. For a non-dividend paying stock, the difference in the value of a put and the value of a call must be equal to the difference between the present value of the exercise price and the stock price S:

$$p - c = Xe^{-r(T-t)} - S \tag{2.15}$$

where p is the value of a European put option on a stock that does not pay dividends. Substituting 2.13 into 2.15 yields:

$$p = Xe^{-r(T-t)}N(d_2) - SN(-d_1), \qquad (2.16)$$

where d_1 and d_2 are as defined above. This equation can also be expressed in a simplified form as:

$$p = p(S,X,r,\sigma^2,\tau), \qquad (2.17)$$

with the following partials:

$$\frac{\partial p}{\partial S} < 0; \quad \frac{\partial p}{\partial X} > 0; \quad \frac{\partial p}{\partial \tau} \underset{<}{>} 0; \quad \frac{\partial p}{\partial \sigma^2} > 0; \quad \frac{\partial p}{\partial r} < 0.$$

Recalling that a put option gives the buyer the right to sell the underlying security at a pre-specified price and time leads to the following intuitive explanation of the above partials. When the stock price falls, an option holder can buy at the lower market price and exercise the option, selling the stock at the higher option exercise price. Therefore, the value of a put option must be inversely related to the price of the underlying stock. A large exercise price increases the likelihood that the market price of the stock will be below the exercise price so the put's value must be directly related to the exercise price. With respect with time to expiration, τ, a longer time to expiration gives the put more time to increase in value which would indicate a positive relationship. However, a European put can only be exercised at expiration, so the buyer has longer to wait before obtaining the exercise price. This would indicate a negative relationship between European put values and time to expiration. According to Chance (1992), the time value effect tends to dominate, meaning that puts with a longer time to expiration will have a larger value. An increase in volatility, σ^2 will affect a put in the same way as a call. A larger volatility means a larger range of prices which increases the probability that the stock's price will be below the exercise price at expiration, thereby increasing the value of the put. Because the put buyer receives the exercise price when exercising the option, a large risk-free rate means a small present value for that exercise price. This indicates a negative relationship between the value of a put and the risk-free rate.

Black and Scholes (1973) conducted empirical tests on their valuation formula and found that actual option prices systematically deviated from the values predicted by their formula. They found that option buyers pay prices that are consistently higher than those predicted by the formula. Option writers were found to receive prices that are close to the level predicted.

The authors also found that the difference between the price paid by option buyers and the value predicted by the formula is greater for options on low-risk stocks than for options on high-risk stocks. Once transactions costs were considered, however, any apparent profit opportunities vanished.

There have been many other studies of the B-S option pricing model in addition to the Black-Scholes (1973) study. Galai (1977) and Bhattacharya (1983) found apparent pricing biases in the basic B-S model. Both of these studies found that when transactions costs were accounted for, however, any arbitrage opportunities vanished.

Black

Recall that the original B-S formula is appropriate for European style options on stocks that do not pay dividends. Black (1975) provided a simple means of adjusting the B-S model to account for known dividends. He pointed out that the dividend payments accruing to a stock are likely to be known with some certainty during the life of an option on that stock. When a stock goes ex-dividend, the value of the stock will go down by an amount equal to the amount of the dividend (or slightly less when adjusted for taxes). When the price of a stock falls, it reduces the likelihood that the stock price will be above the exercise price and, therefore, the likelihood that the option will finish in-the-money. For this reason, an option on a stock that pays dividends will be worth less than an option on an identical stock that does not pay dividends. This is a direct relationship, and the higher the dividend in relation to the stock price, the less the option will be worth.

According to Black, the value of an option on a dividend paying stock which will only be exercised at maturity can be approximated by subtracting the present value of the dividends likely to be paid before maturity from the stock price. This adjusted stock price is used in place of the actual stock price in the standard B-S option pricing model. The present value of the dividends are found by discounting them at whatever interest rate we have assumed for the model.

If the option is American-style however, Merton (1973) has shown that it can sometimes be optimal to exercise the option just before the stock goes ex-dividend. A European call option must be worth at least the stock's price less the present value of the exercise price

$$c \geq S - Xe^{-r(T-t)}$$

However, if a call is in-the-money and is exercised before expiration, the proceeds will be $S - X$. It must be true that $Xe^{-r(T-t)} < X$ for any positive r prior to expiration. Therefore, the option is worth more "alive" than "dead" (dead implying the option had been exercised). Consequently, it will never be rational to exercise an American-style call option on a stock that does not pay dividends prior to the expiration date. It would be better to sell the option than to exercise it. Compared with an equivalent European call option, the American call option offers everything the European option does, plus the opportunity for early exercise. This would imply that $C \geq c$ (where C = American call and c = European call), the difference being the premium for early exercise. In the option pricing literature, this "premium" is referred to as the *early exercise premium*. The above analysis indicates that if the underlying stock does not pay dividends, the early exercise premium is zero and the American call will have the same value as an otherwise identical European call.

It is easy to see how this changes if the stock does pay dividends. Suppose it is very close to the exercise date and a firm's management has just announced a dividend of $25 on a stock whose value is currently $25 (this would be a liquidating dividend) to be paid immediately prior to the option's expiration. Suppose the exercise price on the call is $20. Using the above adjustment procedure, we would replace the current stock price, $25, with the dividend adjusted stock price, $0, and plug into the B-S formula. The call's price will be zero. Therefore it would be optimal to exercise the option prior to the dividend payment. Black (1975) states that the larger the dividend and the closer the payment to the expiration date, the more likely it is to be optimal for early exercise of the option.

Black (1975) first proposed a way to account for the possibility of early exercise through a process called pseudo-American call option pricing. Black suggests figuring an alternative value of the option by assuming that it expires just before the last ex-dividend date, t_n. If this value is higher value than the European value, then it should be used as the true option price.

The steps in deriving the price of an option on a stock that pays dividends an which can be exercised early involve first subtracting the present value of all dividends that will be paid before the option expires from the stock price. Next, for each dividend date, subtract the present value of all dividends yet to be paid from the option's exercise price. Next use the B-S model to compute European option prices using each dividend date and the actual expiration date as possible expiration dates. The highest of the computed European prices should be the estimate for the American call's price.

Merton

Merton (1973) developed a derivation of the basic B-S model that is suitable for pricing European-style options on foreign exchange (FX), options on futures and stock index options. He shows how to adjust the B-S model to account for continuous dividends where the dividend rate is treated as a negative interest rate. For the pricing of FX options, the continuous dividend is the foreign interest rate. As mentioned earlier, the payment of dividends reduces the value of the underlying stock and hence the value of a call option on that asset. This reduction for constant dividends is often called "leakage" and is typically represented in Merton's model as δ. Merton's model for continuous dividends is given as:

$$c^M = e^{-\delta(T-t)} SN\left(d_1^M\right) - Xe^{-r(T-t)} N\left(d_2^M\right) \qquad (2.18)$$

$$d_1^M = \frac{\ln\left(\dfrac{S}{X}\right) + \left(r - \delta + \dfrac{\sigma^2}{2}\right)(T-t)}{\sigma\sqrt{T-t}} \qquad (2.18a)$$

$$d_2^M = d_1^M - \sigma\sqrt{T-t} \qquad (2.18b)$$

where δ is the continuous dividend rate on the stock.
When the dividend rate is zero, Merton's model reduces to the
original B-S option pricing model. The adjusted put value calculated by
Merton is

$$p^M = Xe^{-r(T-t)}N\left(d_2^M\right) - Se^{-\delta(T-t)}N\left(-d_1^M\right). \tag{2.19}$$

For pricing FX options replace S with the dollar value of the foreign
currency, let δ be the foreign interest rate and the standard deviation is
that of the foreign currency.

Earlier it was mentioned that the basis B-S model was derived
under the assumption of a constant interest rate. Merton (1973) has also
developed a model that accounts for the possibility of a stochastic
interest rate. Merton defines $B(t)$ as the value of a discount bond that
matures at the same time as the option and which has a payoff of $1 at
maturity. It is assumed that B follows a process similar to that of the
stock as

$$\frac{dB}{B} = \mu_B dt + \sigma_B dz_B \tag{2.20}$$

where μ_B = the growth rate in the bond price, σ_B = the volatility of B,
dz_B is a Wiener process, and μ_B is stochastic. Merton the follows an
analysis similar to that of the B-S analysis outlined earlier in this
chapter to derive the following European call price as:

$$c = SN\left(d_1\right) - BXN\left(d_2\right) \tag{2.21}$$

$$d_1 = \frac{\ln\left(\frac{S}{X}\right) - \ln B + \left(\frac{\sigma^2}{2}\right)(T-t)}{\sigma\sqrt{T-t}} \tag{2.21a}$$

$$d_2 = d_1 - \sigma\sqrt{T-t} \tag{2.21b}$$

$$\sigma\sqrt{T-t} = \int_t^T \left(\sigma^2 + \sigma_B^2 - 2\rho\sigma\sigma_B\right)dt \tag{2.21c}$$

where σ = the stock's volatility and ρ = the instantaneous correlation between the stock and bond prices, and $B = e^{-R(T-t)}$. Here R is the rate of interest on a risk-free bond whose maturity coincides with the options expiration date. Therefore, this model is a derivation of the B-S model with R and σ' replacing r and σ. According to Hull and White (1990), one of the criticisms of this model is that the volatility of the discount bond is a known function of time. More complex models of interest rates such as that proposed by Vasicek (1977) and Cox, Ingersoll, and Ross (1985) set the volatility of bond prices as a function of time and the bond price.

SECTION II: OPTION PRICING USING ANALYTICAL METHODS

Cox and Ross

Cox and Ross (1975) introduced an option pricing model known as the *pure jump model*, and this model was further elaborated on in Cox, Ross and Rubinstein (1979). The models examined so far have assumed that options follow some continuous path. With the pure jump model, the stock price follows a jump process as

$$\frac{dS}{S} = \mu dt + (k-1)d\pi \qquad (2.22)$$

where π is a continuous-time Poisson[3] process and $k - 1$ is the jump amplitude. The stock price has two components: a drift term, μdt and the term $d\pi$ which has a probability of λdt of jumping the percentage stock change to $k - 1$ and a probability of $1 - \lambda dt$ of doing nothing. This model is rather unrealistic, however, in the fact that the stock price can only jump up.

Merton

Merton (1976) developed a model that can be considered a combination of a model that assumes a continuous process for the stock and a pure jump model. The model is known as the jump-diffusion model. Merton defines the following stock price process

$$\frac{dS}{S} = (\mu - \lambda k)dt + \sigma dz + dq \qquad (2.23)$$

where dz is a standard Wiener process, dq is the Poisson process which generates the jumps, σ is the standard deviation of the Wiener process, μ is the expected return on the stock, λ is the rate at which jumps happen, k is the average jump size, and dz and dq are independent. According to Merton, the jump component is not priced in the economy and the formula for a European call option is given as

$$c = \sum_{n=0}^{\infty} \frac{e^{-\lambda \tau}(\lambda \tau)^n}{n!} f_n \qquad (2.24)$$

where $\lambda' = \lambda(1 + k)$, $\tau = T - t$, and f_n is the B-S option price after making adjustments to the risk-free rate and the instantaneous variance. The risk-free rate in the standard B-S model is adjusted by adding the term

$$\frac{n \ln(1+k)}{T-t} - \lambda k$$

to the risk-free rate, r, and the instantaneous variance is adjusted by adding the term

$$\frac{n\delta^2}{T-t}$$

to the variance, σ^2.

Geske

Geske (1979) developed a procedure to price compound options. He noted that if the equity on a levered firm is viewed as an option, then an option on that equity is really an option on an option (a compound option). He also noted that the B-S model's pricing biases may be a result of that model's inability to price such options accurately.

In order to show why an option is really a compound option, suppose we have a firm that has been financed with common stock and a single pure discount bond due to mature in one year. Assume the bond has a face value $= B_1$, that the current time is $t = 0$, the bond's maturity date is $t = 1$, and that the firm will generate some form of cash flows between $t = 0$ and $t = 1$. The value of the firm at time zero will be $V_0 = S_0 + B_0$, where S and B represent the value of the outstanding stocks and debt, respectively, at time $t = 0$. The variable B_0 is the present value of the face value of the bonds due to retire at time $t = 1$, discounted at some discount rate r. Therefore $B_0 = B_1 e^{-r(1)}$. At maturity, if the firm has sufficient cash flows, it can pay off its indebtedness, B_1. If the firm does not have sufficient cash flows to cover its debt, it defaults, and the bondholders take over and try to salvage what they can. Therefore, the payoff at time $t = 1$ for the stock holders will be $S_1 = MAX[0, V_1 - B_1]$. This shows that the stock can be thought of as a call option on the firm whose exercise price is the face value of the firm's debt, implying that an option on a firm's stock is really an option on a option or a compound option.

Following Geske, the B-S model can be used to derive the value of the firm's stock as

$$S = VN(d_1) - Be^{-r(T-t)} N(d_2) \qquad (2.25)$$

$$d_1 = \frac{\ln\left(\dfrac{V}{B}\right) + \left(r + \dfrac{\sigma_V^2}{2}\right)(T-t)}{\sigma_2 \sqrt{T-t}} \qquad (2.25a)$$

$$d_2 = d_1 - \sigma_V \sqrt{T-t} \qquad (2.25b)$$

where V is the value of the firm, B is the face value of the firm's debt, σ_V is the volatility of V, and all the debt is assumed to mature at time T. The firm's debt and the volatility are assumed constant. Geske's compound option pricing model for a European-style call option on a stock that does not pay dividends is given as

$$c_G = VM\left(\alpha_1, \varsigma_1; \sqrt{\frac{\tau_1}{\tau_2}}\right) - Be^{-r\tau_2} M\left(\alpha_2, \varsigma_2; \sqrt{\frac{\tau_1}{\tau_2}}\right) - Xe^{-r\tau_1} N(\alpha_2) \quad (2.26)$$

$$\alpha_1 = \frac{\ln\left(\dfrac{V}{V^*}\right) + \left(r + \dfrac{\sigma_V^2}{2}\right)\tau_1}{\sigma_V\sqrt{\tau_1}}$$

$$\varsigma_1 = \frac{\ln\left(\dfrac{V}{B}\right) + \left(r + \dfrac{\sigma_V^2}{2}\right)\tau_2}{\sigma_V\sqrt{\tau_2}}$$

$$\alpha_2 = \alpha_1 - \sigma_V\sqrt{\tau_1}$$

$$\varsigma_2 = \varsigma_1 - \sigma_V\sqrt{\tau_2}$$

$$\tau_1 = T - t$$

$$\tau_2 = T^* - t$$

where V^* is the value of the firm at time T. T^* is the maturity date for the firm's debt while T is the option's expiration date. Following Geske, the function $M(\alpha,\varsigma;\gamma)$ is the cumulative probability in a standardized bivariate normal distribution that the first variable is less than α and the second variable is less than ς when the coefficient of correlation between the variables is γ. This function has to be evaluated analytically. Geske's model can be used to evaluate any of the four basic types of compound options: call on a call, call on a put, put on a put, and put on a call. Although more complex than the B-S model due to the fact that the face value of the debt and the maturity of the debt must be obtained, this model does not require the assumption of a constant variance.

Cox, Ross, and Rubinstein

Cox, Ross, and Rubinstein (1979) developed the binomial option pricing model (BOPM). This model was also developed independently by Rendleman and Bartter (1979). The BOPM model uses the same parameters to price options as does the B-S OPM (stock price, exercise price, time to expiration, interest rate, and volatility) and was derived using the same arbitrage principals as B-S. The main difference in the two models is that in the BOPM the time to expiration is partitioned into discrete intervals of equal length. In each period the stock price can either increase or decrease (follows a binomial process). The B-S model is a continuous time model. As the number of time period approaches infinity for the BOPM (alternatively, as the time interval becomes smaller), the BOPM converges to the B-S model. As with the B-S model, the BOPM is appropriate only for European-style options that do not pay dividends. Adjustments to the model must be made to account for early exercise and dividends.

Although Cox, Ross, and Rubinstein provide a rather detailed derivation of the BOPM, a simpler approach is provided by Kolb (1994, pp. 486-497). For this reason, Kolb's explanation of the BOPM is provided here.

In deriving the BOPM it will be assumed that the capital market is frictionless and competitive to preclude riskless arbitrage. For now, only a one period process will be assumed (where the period can be a year, quarter, month, etc.). Different from the B-S analysis however, the stock price, S, will be assumed to follow a binomial process. Suppose the stock price today is $S = \$50$, and that in one period, time = T, the stock price will either be \$60 or \$42.50. The term, u, then can be defined as the multiplicative upward movement in the stock price as $u = \$60/\$50 = 1.2$. The term, d, can be defined as the multiplicative downward movement in the stock price as $d = \$42.50/\$50 = .85$. In order to preclude the stock price from going below \$0, $d < 1$. Let r equal the risk-free rate where $r = .10$ for this example. In order to preclude arbitrage requires that $u > 1 + r > d$. Further, suppose the probability of an increase is denoted as ρ, and $1 - \rho$ is the probability of a decrease. The one-period binomial stock process is given in figure 2.1.

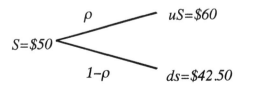

Figure 2.1

Now suppose there is a call option, c, whose strike price, X, is $50 written on the above stock. The payoff on the call at time T will be MAX[0,$uS - X$] = MAX[0,$10]. So there is a equal probability of the call paying $0 or $10 at expiration. Figure 2.2 shows the payoffs for the call option.

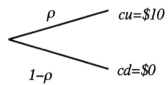

Figure 2.2

This is simple, but we are concerned with what the call is worth today. This can be found by constructing a synthetic option, namely a portfolio, P_R, that has the same payoffs as the call option above. This portfolio will consist of h shares of stock bought at today's price, S, and a short position in a risk-free bond, B, that matures at T. We are basically borrowing B at the risk-free rate, r. At time T, we will have to pay back $(1+r)B$. The value of this portfolio today is

$$P_R = hS - B. \tag{2.27}$$

At time T, the portfolio will have a value of

$$c_u = huS - (1+r)B \tag{2.28}$$

$$c_d = hdS - (1+r)B. \tag{2.29}$$

The payoffs for this portfolio are depicted in figure 2.3 below.

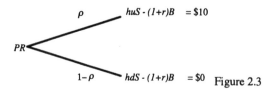

Figure 2.3

These are the same payoffs as for the call option, c. Equations 2.29 and 2.30 above can be used to solve for the values of h and B as follows:

$$h^* = \frac{c_u - c_d}{uS - dS} \tag{2.30}$$

$$B^* = \frac{c_u(dS) - c_d(uS)}{(1 + r)(uS - dS)}. \tag{2.31}$$

Using our example:

$$h^* = \frac{c_u - c_d}{uS - dS} = \frac{\$10 - \$0}{\$60 - \$42.50} = .5714$$

$$B^* = \frac{c_u(dS) - c_d(uS)}{(1 + r)(uS - dS)} = \frac{\$10(\$42.50) - \$0(\$60)}{(1.10)(\$60 - \$42.50)} = \$22.08.$$

Therefore, our portfolio consists of .5714 shares of stock purchased at $50 and borrowings at the risk-free rate of .10 of $22.08. The end of period payoffs for this portfolio are:

$$uP_R = (.5714)(\$60) - (1.10)(\$22.08) = \$10$$

$$dP_R = (.5714)(\$42.50) - (1.10)(\$22.08) = \$0.$$

These are the same payoffs as for the call option. In a rational world, two securities with the same risk and cash-flows should have the same price. Therefore, the value of the call, c, must be equal to the value of the portfolio, P_R so that

$$c^* = h^* S - B^*. \tag{2.32}$$

This is the single-period binomial call pricing model. It shows the value of the call is equal to the value of a long position in the stock less some borrowing at the risk free rate. Using our numbers above, the value of the call option today is

$$c^* = (.5714)(\$50) - \$22.08 = \$6.49.$$

Using the put-call parity relation, the value of a put option on the above stock can be calculated as

$$p^* = c^* + \left(\frac{X}{(1+r)}\right) - S = \$6.49 + \frac{\$50}{(1.10)} - \$50 = \$1.95.$$

Thus far the probability of a stock price movement has been ignored. We can account for these probabilities by assuming a risk-neutral world and substituting the values for h* (Eq. 2.31) and B* (Eq. 2.32) into the value of a call (Eq. 2.33) which gives

$$c = \left(\frac{c_u - c_d}{uS - dS}\right) S - \frac{c_u(dS) - c_d(uS)}{(1+r)(uS - dS)}.$$ (2.33)

After substituting $R = 1 + r$, we can simplify and rearrange to isolate c_u and c_d which gives

$$c = \frac{\left(\frac{R-d}{u-d}\right)c_u + \left(\frac{u-R}{u-d}\right)c_d}{R}.$$ (2.34)

Expressed this way, the value of the call is the present value of the future payoffs and the probability of a stock price increase is also the probability that the call will be worth c_u. In other words, the probability of an upward price movement is

$$\rho_u = \frac{R-d}{u-d},$$ (2.35)

and the probability of a downward price movement is

$$\rho_d = \frac{u-R}{u-d} = 1 - \rho_u.$$ (2.36)

Using our numbers from the above example, the probability of a stock price increase is

$$\rho_u = \frac{1.1 - .85}{1.2 - .85} = .7143,$$

and the probability of a stock price decrease is

$$\rho_d = 1 - .7143 = .2857.$$

These probabilities can be substituted into Eq. 2.35 to find the value of the call as

$$c^* = \frac{\rho_u c_u + \rho_d c_d}{R} = \frac{(.7143)(\$10) + (.2857)(\$0)}{1.1} = \$6.49,$$

which is the same as was derived above. One of the interesting points of the BOPM is that the probability of an upward price movement in the stock is not needed when calculating the option value. The BOPM gives the value of the call as the expected value of the call's payoff at expiration, discounted at the risk-free rate and assuming risk-neutrality.

This model is lacking because it only accounts for one period. Suppose we were looking at two periods. The stock's binomial tree is represented in Figure 2.4.

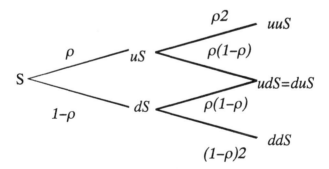

Figure 2.4

The option will have a specific value associated with each terminal stock price. Figure 2.5 shows the binomial tree for the call option.

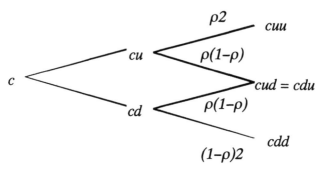

Figure 2.5

If the stock price increases in both periods, the resulting price is uuS, and c_{uu} is the call option price if the stock price goes up on both periods. Therefore, ρ_{uu} is the probability that there will be an increase in the stock price for both periods. Because the call value is equal to the expected two-period payoffs discounted at the risk-free rate, we can extend Equation 2.35 to account for two periods

$$c = \frac{\rho_{uu}c_{uu} + \rho_{ud}c_{ud} + \rho_{du}c_{du} + \rho_{dd}c_{dd}}{R^2}. \tag{2.37}$$

Continuing with the previous example, the value of the two-period call option can be computed as

$$c^* = \frac{(.5102)(\$22) + (.2041)(\$1) + (.2041)(\$1) + (.0816)(\$0)}{(1.10)^2} = \$9.61,$$

and applying the put-call parity equation gives a put value of \$.94.

From here, the BOPM is easily extended to n periods as

$$c = \frac{\displaystyle\sum_{j=k}^{n} \left(\frac{n!}{j!(n-j)!}\right)\left[\rho_u^j \rho_d^{n-j}\right] MAX\left[0, u^j d^{n-j} S - X\right]}{R^n}. \tag{2.38}$$

Equation 2.39 is the complete expression for the binomial option pricing model. When j = 0, the stock price never rises. When j = n, the stock price rises every period.

The model in Equation 2.39 can be re-written in order to compare it to the B-S option pricing model which was derived earlier. The first step in doing so is to recognize that we are only concerned with those option values that are in-the-money (c>$0). Let k be defined as the minimum number of times the stock price must rise in order to finish in-the-money. Then over n periods, if the stock price rises k times, it falls $n-k$ times. In computing the option value, we need only concern ourselves with those values from $j = k$ to $j = n$. Following this line of reasoning, equation 2.29 can be re-written as

$$c = \frac{\sum_{j=k}^{n} \left(\frac{n!}{j!(n-j)!} \right) \left[\rho_u^j \rho_d^{n-j} \right] \left[u^j d^{n-j} S - X \right]}{R^n}.$$

(2.39)

Next, we can break Equation 2.39 into two parts as

$$c = \left[\sum_{j=k}^{n} \left(\frac{n!}{j!(n-j)!} \right) \left(\rho_u^j \rho_d^{n-j} \right) \left(\frac{u^j d^{n-j}}{R^n} \right) \right] S$$

(2.40)

$$-XR^{-n} = \left[\sum_{j=k}^{n} \left(\frac{n!}{j!(n-j)!} \right) \rho_u^j \rho_d^{n-j} \right]$$

Following Copeland and Weston (1988), the first term in Equation 2.41 is the stock price, S, multiplied by a complementary binomial distribution B(j ≥ k|n,ρ_d); and the second term is the discounted value of the exercise price, XR^{-n} multiplied by a complementary binomial distribution B(j ≥ k|n,ρ_u). According to Copeland and Weston (1989), the complementary binomial probability is the cumulative probability of having in-the-money options. In other words, B(j ≥ k|n,ρ_u) is the complementary binomial probability that j ≥ k. Equation 2.40 can therefore be expressed as

$$c = SB\left(j \geq k | n, \rho_d \right) - XR^{-n} B\left(j \geq k | n, \rho_u \right).$$

(2.41)

Viewed this way, it is easy to see how the call value is affected by the state variables. As the stock price, S, increases, the value of the call increases. There is an inverse relationship between the strike price, X, and the call value. As the risk-free rate increases, $R = (1 + r)$ increases which leads to a decrease in the discounted value of the strike price. This in turn leads to a higher call value. The mean (expected value) and variance of the binomial distribution are $\mu = E(j) = n\rho$ and $\sigma^2 = VAR(j) = n\rho(1 - \rho)$. As n grows large, the number of possible option values increases, and therefore the number of in-the-money payoffs increase. Using the mean of the binomial, as n increases $E(j)$ increases and therefore the value of the call increases. Finally, an increase in the binomial variance has a positive impact on the call's value. This is because an increase in the binomial variance will result if the size of the stock price change increases. This increases the likelihood that the stock price will exceed the strike price and therefore increases the likelihood that the option finishes in-the-money.

When examining the BOPM, an increase in n does not necessarily imply a longer time horizon (e.g. 3 months to 6 months), but may instead imply a larger number of equal width time intervals within some period $T - t$. For example, a year can be considered a unit which can be subdivided into 12 months, 52 weeks, 365 days, 8,760 hours, etc. In general, as the number of binomial trials is increased for some fixed time interval $T - t$, the more accurate will be the computed binomial price. Although the BOPM is a discrete time model, as the period $T - t$ is divided into smaller and smaller intervals, $n \rightarrow \infty$ and the model becomes a continuous one. In fact, Cox, Ross, and Rubinstein (1979) have shown that as $n \rightarrow \infty$, $B(j \geq k|n,\rho_u) \rightarrow N(d_1)$ and $B(j \geq k|n,\rho_d) \rightarrow N(d_2)$, where $N(\cdot)$ is the cumulative normal distribution function. The authors also show that $(1 + r)^{-(T-t)} \rightarrow e^{-r(T-t)}$ as the number of intervals, n, within the period $T - t$ grows very large. Substituting these limits into Equation 2.41 gives

$$c = SN(d_1) - Xe^{-r(T-t)}N(d_2)$$

which is the B-S option pricing formula derived in Equation 2.13. Therefore, the B-S model can be seen as a limiting case of the BOPM.

The analysis for the BOPM has been for call options on European-style options. When the authors computed a put value, they have used the put-call parity relation. However, it is easy to price puts using the BOPM. Simply replace the call payoffs at expiration with put payoffs and use the same formulas, replacing c's with p's. Recalling that k was defined as the minimum number of times that the stock price must rise for a call option to be in the money, then it must be true that a put option will be in the money if the stock rises fewer than k times. Therefore, the value of the put option is given as

$$p = \frac{\sum_{j=0}^{k-1} \left(\frac{n!}{j!(n-j)!} \right) \left[\rho_u^j \rho_d^{n-j} \right] \left[X - u^j d^{n-j} S \right]}{R^n}. \tag{2.42}$$

As with the B-S model, the BOPM is appropriate only for non-dividend European-style options. If the option is American, or if the option is written on a dividend paying stock, adjustments must be made. Fortunately, adjustments for dividends on the BOPM are simple. The BOPM can be adjusted for continuous dividends, known dividend yields, and known dollar dividend yields by adjusting the stock price throughout the binomial tree to account for dividends. Once the stock price has been adjusted to account for dividends, the option price is computed in the usual way.

Barone-Adesi and Whaley

There is no closed form solution to the value of an American call option on a dividend paying stock with one exception. When a stock is expected to pay one known dividend during the life of the option, the compound option pricing model can be used to compute an exact price for said option. For other American options, such as options on an underlying instrument that pays a continuous dividend, there is no closed form solution. Therefore, some approximation technique must be used. Barone-Adesi and Whaley (1987) develop an analytic approximation for pricing exchange-traded American call and put options written on commodities and commodity futures contracts (such options are considered to be options on underlying securities that pay a continuous dividend).

The authors begin their analysis by reviewing Merton's (1973) continuous European option pricing model. It is assumed that the short-term interest rate, r, and the cost of carrying the commodity, b, are constant, proportional rates. The Merton model can then be applied to a number of situations. If the underlying security is a non-dividend paying security, the cost of carry will be equal to the risk-free rate ($b = r$), but this will not always be the case. If the underlying security is a stock paying a continuous dividend, the cost of carrying the stock will be the risk-free rate less the dividend yield ($b = r - d$). If the underlying security is a foreign currency, the cost of carrying the foreign currency is the domestic risk-free rate less the foreign risk-free rate, r^f,($b = r - r^f$). For traditional agricultural commodities, the cost of carry will exceed the risk-free rate by costs of storage, insurance, and deterioration.

Under the assumption of a constant proportional cost of carry, the relationship between futures and underlying commodity prices is

$$F = Se^{b(T-t)} \qquad (2.43)$$

where F and S are the futures and spot prices of the underlying commodity, respectively. For financial securities and precious metals, the relationship is $F = S^{r(T-t)}$, where r is the risk-free rate and can also be thought of as the rate at which the spot price grows. It is also assumed that the underlying commodity follows the process

$$\frac{dS}{S} = \mu dt + \sigma dw \qquad (2.44)$$

where:

   S = initial commodity price.

   μ = the instantaneous expected rate of return on the commodity.

   σ = the instantaneous standard deviation of the rate of return.

   dw = a standard Wiener process.

   dt = some small increment of time.

If the cost-of-carry equation 2.43 holds and if the commodity's price movements can be described by 2.44, then the movement of the futures price can be described by

$$\frac{dF}{F} = (\mu - b)dt + \sigma dw. \tag{2.45}$$

According to Baroni-Adesi and Whaley, this implies that the expected instantaneous relative price change of the futures contract is $\mu - b$ and the standard deviation of relative commodity price relatives is equal to the standard deviation of futures price relatives.

If some security, c, is dependent on the underlying commodity price, S, and time, t, then it follows from Ito's lemma that

$$dc = \frac{\partial c}{\partial S}dS + \frac{\partial c}{\partial t}dt + \frac{1}{2}\frac{\partial^2 c}{\partial S^2}\sigma^2 S^2 dt \tag{2.46}$$

and substituting for dS gives

$$dc = \left(\frac{\partial c}{\partial S}\sigma S + \frac{\partial c}{\partial t}dt + \frac{1}{2}\frac{\partial^2 c}{\partial S^2}\sigma^2 S^2\right)dt + \frac{\partial c}{\partial S}\sigma Sw. \tag{2.47}$$

From this point, a riskless hedge portfolio is formed consisting of -1 of the derivative securities and $\partial c/\partial S$ of the underlying commodity, S. If the value of such a portfolio is defined as V such that $V = -c + (\partial c/\partial S)S$, then the change in that portfolio's value over time Δt will be

$$\Delta V = \Delta c + \frac{\partial c}{\partial S}\Delta S. \tag{2.48}$$

Equations 2.45 and 2.47 can be re-written in their discrete time formats and substituted into equation 2.48. Doing so and simplifying yields

$$\Delta V = -\frac{\partial c}{\partial t}\Delta t - \frac{1}{2}\frac{\partial^2 c}{\partial S^2}\sigma^2 S^2 \Delta t. \tag{2.49}$$

Over time Δt, the holder of the above portfolio will gain $b(\partial c/\partial S)S\Delta t$, where b can be thought of as the rate at which the spot price grows (or the continuous dividend if referring to a stock that pays a continuous dividend), therefore the change in wealth for the portfolio holder can be represented by

$$\Delta Wealth = -\frac{\partial c}{\partial t}\Delta t - \frac{1}{2}\frac{\partial^2 c}{\partial S^2}\sigma^2 S^2 \Delta t + b\frac{\partial c}{\partial S}S\Delta t. \qquad (2.50)$$

Because the portfolio is riskless over time Δt, the change in wealth must be equal to the return that could have been earned if the investment in the portfolio had instead been invested at the risk-free rate, r. By setting equation 2.50 equal to $rV\Delta t$ (the return that would have been earned had the amount V been invested at the risk-free rate) and substituting for V, the following p.d.e. representing the movement of the option on the commodity can be derived

$$\frac{\partial c}{\partial t} + \frac{1}{2}\frac{\partial^2 c}{\partial S^2}\sigma^2 S^2 + (r-b)\frac{\partial c}{\partial S}S - rc = 0. \qquad (2.51)$$

Equation 2.51 is similar to that derived by Merton and is the basis for the analysis of Baroni-Adesi and Whaley.

Baroni-Adesi and Whaley show that when the terminal boundary conditions of MAX(0,S − X) and MAX(X−S, 0) are applied to the p.d.e. in 2.51 for European call and put options respectively, the following call and put option values are derived:

$$c^M = e^{-b(T-t)}SN\left(d_1^M\right) - Xe^{-r(T-t)}N\left(d_2^M\right) \qquad (2.52)$$

$$p^M = Xe^{-r(T-t)}N\left(-d_2^M\right) - Se^{-b(T-t)}N\left(-d_1^M\right). \qquad (2.53)$$

where

$$d_1^M = \frac{\ln\left(\frac{S}{X}\right) + \left(r - b + \frac{\sigma^2}{2}\right)(T - t)}{\sigma\sqrt{T-t}}$$

$$d_2^M = d_1^M - \sigma\sqrt{T-t}$$

which are the Merton call and put option pricing formulae. Notice that if $b = 0$ (as would be the case for a stock paying no dividends), the above formulae collapse into the basic B-S formulae. In the case where $r = b$ (as would be the case for many financial futures and futures on precious metals), the formulae become much simpler.

Baroni-Adesi and Whaley use the above European call formula to explain how, under certain conditions, an American call option may be exercised early. They point out that for most non-common-stock commodity options traded the cost of carry will be less than the risk-free rate ($b < r$). If the commodity price, S, becomes very large, $N(d_1{}^M)$ and $N(d_2{}^M)$ will both approach one, and the value of a European call will approach $Se^{(b-r)(T-t)} - Xe^{-r(T-t)}$. The American call may be exercised immediately for $S - X$, which may be higher than the European price when $b < r$. For an option on a non-dividend-paying stock, the cost of carry will equal the risk-free rate ($b = r$); and for situations when $b \geq r$, there will be no early exercise because the lower bound for the European option will be greater than the value of an otherwise equivalent American option. In such a situation, the European model (equation 2.52) applies. For puts, there will always be a probability of early exercise and the European model will be inappropriate.

Baroni-Adesi and Whaley posit that the valuation of American commodity options involves addressing the early exercise feature of the options and approximation methods must be used. The authors point out that the most common analytical method involves finite-difference methods utilized by Schwartz (1977), Brennan and Schwartz (1977), Ramaswamy and Sundaresan (1985), and Brenner, Courtadon, and Subrahmanyam (1985). According to the authors, finite difference methods are computationally inefficient, requiring a main-frame computer to provide efficient results. Considering the power of today's desktop computers, one can no longer be sure if this argument holds.

Although it is argued that the compound-option approximation introduced by Geske and Johnson (1984) is computationally less cumbersome than finite difference methods, the model still requires the evaluation of cumulative bivariate, trivariate, and sometimes higher order multivariate normal density functions. The authors point out that such evaluations are still computationally unwieldy.

Because of the shortcomings of the above mentioned methods, Baroni-Adesi and Whaley develop a model (hereafter referred to as the BAW model) based on MacMillan's (1986) quadratic approximation of the American put option. The authors note that if the p.d.e. (2.51) applies to American options as well as European options, it also applies to the early exercise premium of the American option. Therefore, the early exercise premium can be represented as

$$\varepsilon_c = C(S) - c(S) \tag{2.54}$$

where c(S) is the European commodity option value and C(S) is the American commodity option value. The p.d.e. for the early exercise premium can then be derived as

$$\frac{\partial \varepsilon}{\partial t} + \frac{1}{2}\frac{\partial^2 \varepsilon}{\partial S^2}\sigma^2 S^2 + (r-b)\frac{\partial \varepsilon}{\partial S}S - r\varepsilon = 0. \tag{2.55}$$

To simplify, the authors define $\tau = T - t$, $M = 2r/\sigma^2$, $N = 2(r-b)/\sigma^2$, $K(\tau) = 1 - e^{-r\tau}$, and the early exercise premium is defined as $\varepsilon_C = K(\tau)f(\tau,K)$ and re-write equation 2.55 as

$$S^2\frac{\partial^2 f}{\partial S^2} + NS\frac{\partial f}{\partial S} - \frac{M}{K}f = 0. \tag{2.56}$$

The authors state that equation 2.56 "is a second-order ordinary differential equation with two linearly independent solutions of the form AS^q." The solutions are found by substituting $f = AS^q$ into 2.56

$$AS^q = \left[q^2 + (N-1)q - \frac{M}{K}\right] = 0. \tag{2.57}$$

The roots of equation 2.57 are

$$q_1 = \frac{-(N-1) - \sqrt{(N-1)^2 + 4\frac{M}{K}}}{2},$$

and

$$q_2 = \frac{-(N-1) + \sqrt{(N-1)^2 + 4\frac{M}{K}}}{2}.$$

Therefore, the general solution to 2.56 is

$$f(S) = A_1 S^{q1} + A_2 S^{q2}.$$

From this point, the authors apply boundary conditions for the American call and put and derive the following American call option pricing formulae

$$C(S) = c(S) + A_{21}\left(S/S^*\right)q_2 \quad \text{when } S < S*$$
$$= S - X \quad \text{when } S \geq S*$$

where $S*$ is the critical commodity price. If the current commodity price is above this critical price, an American call should be exercised. If the current commodity price is below the critical price, an American put should be exercised. The critical commodity price must be solved for iteratively using

$$S* - X = c(S*) + \frac{\left[1 - e^{-b\tau} N\left(d_1^*\right)\right] S*}{q_2} \tag{2.58}$$

where $c(S*)$ is the B-S value calculated when $S*$ is the commodity price and $N(d_1*)$ is the cumulative normal probability computed using $S*$. The value for a put option is given as

$$P(S) = p(S) + A_1\left(S/S**\right)q_1 \quad \text{when } S > S**$$
$$= X - S \quad \text{when } S \leq S**$$

where $p(S)$ is the B-S put option value and $S**$ is the critical commodity price below which the American put option should be exercised. This critical price is found iteratively by solving

$$X - S** = p(S**) - \frac{\left[1 - e^{-b\tau} N\left(-d_1^{**}\right)\right] S**}{q_1} \tag{2.59}$$

where $p(S**)$ is the B-S value of the put option when the commodity price is $S**$ and $N(-d_1**)$ is computed using $S**$.

Baroni-Adesi and Whaley point out that the BAW model is appropriate for options on stock indices, currencies, futures contracts and options on a stock paying a continuous dividend. The authors perform a number of simulations and compare the BAW with the European, finite-difference approximation and the compound-option pricing approximation methods. The finite-difference approximation method was assumed to provide the "true" value of an American option. Their conclusions are:

1. When pricing commodity options and commodity futures options, the BAW provides results that are very close to the finite-difference method; and although the compound option valuation method provides good results also, the computational cost of the BAW is about 100 times less than that of the compound option approximation.

2. When pricing long-term options, the BAW model encounters difficulty. The authors recommend using the BAW model for options with maturities of less than one year and using finite-difference or binomial option pricing methods for options with expirations beyond one year.

SECTION III: OPTIONS ON FUTURES, CURRENCIES AND INDICES

Merton

With options on stock indices, currencies and futures contracts, the underlying security (a stock index or a S&P 500 futures contract for example) can be thought of as a stock paying a continuous dividend. Merton (1973) shows how to adjust the B-S model to account for continuous dividends where the dividend rate is treated as a negative interest rate. As mentioned in Section I above, this makes Merton's model suitable for pricing European-style options on foreign exchange (FX), options on futures and stock index options. Merton's model for continuous dividends was provided in equations 2.18–2.19 and is repeated here for convenience.

$$c^M = e^{-\delta(T-t)} S N\left(d_1^M\right) - X e^{-r(T-t)} N\left(d_2^M\right) \qquad (2.18)$$

$$d_1^M = \frac{\ln\left(\frac{S}{X}\right) + \left(r - \delta + \frac{\sigma^2}{2}\right)(T - t)}{\sigma\sqrt{T - t}} \qquad (2.18a)$$

$$d_2^M = d_1^M - \sigma\sqrt{T - t} \qquad (2.18b)$$

where δ is the continuous dividend rate on the stock. When the dividend rate is zero, Merton's model reduces to the original B-S option pricing model. The adjusted put value calculated by Merton is

$$p^M = Xe^{-r(T-t)}N\left(-d_2^M\right) - Se^{-\delta(T-t)}N\left(-d_1^M\right). \qquad (2.19)$$

For pricing FX options, replace S with the dollar value of the foreign currency, let δ be the foreign interest rate and the standard deviation is that of the foreign currency.

The returns on a stock index are a combination of the capital gains and dividend payments of the stocks making up the index. Although individual stocks pay dividends discretely, it is justifiable to think of a large index (such as the S&P 500) as paying a constant dividend. This being the case, one can simply replace S with the current index value, let δ be the continuous dividend rate on the index and the standard deviation is that of the index.

With options on futures (futures options) a call option gives the buyer the right, but not the obligation, to take a long position in the futures market. A put option gives the buyer the right, but not the obligation, to take a short position in the futures market. Futures prices on precious metals and financial instruments are determined by the following relationship:

$$F_t = S_t^{\alpha(T-t)} \qquad (2.60)$$

where F_t is the futures price at time t, S_t is the spot price of the underlying security at time t, and α is the rate at which the spot price grows. This is known as the cost-of-carry model (see any standard Futures textbook, e.g. Kolb[1994]). To use Merton's model to price futures contracts, replace the futures price with the stock price and δ

with α in equations 2.19, 2.19a, 2.19b and 2.20 above. For financial assets, α is the risk-free rate of interest minus the yield on the asset. In this case, the futures contract can be thought of as a stock paying a continuous dividend equal to r and the above formulas can be simplified by replacing δ with r.

The above adjustments to the Merton model are not unique. The BOPM model for continuous dividends mentioned in Section II above can also be used to price European options on indices, currencies and futures contracts. Because dividend payments are actually discrete (usually occurring quarterly), the BOPM is well-suited for pricing European-style stock index options.

Black

Black (1976) used assumptions similar to those in deriving the original B-S formula to find values for commodity options in terms of futures prices and other variables. He assumes that futures prices are determined by the relationship in equation 2.60 above, that α is only a function of time, and that the volatility of the futures contract is constant and equal to the volatility of the underlying commodity. It is also assumed that the underlying commodity follows a process similar to that in equation 2.1 of Section I above. The remaining assumptions of the original B-S derivation apply.

Under these assumptions, the futures price can be said to follow the process

$$dF = \mu F dt + \sigma F dw \tag{2.61}$$

where:

F = initial stock price.

μ = the instantaneous expected rate of return on the futures contract.

σ = the instantaneous standard deviation of the rate of return.

dw = a standard Wiener process.

dt = some small increment of time.

Black creates a riskless hedge by simultaneously taking a long position in one contract and a short position in the other contract. Suppose a short position is taking on the option, -c, and a long position is taken on the futures contract equal to $\partial c/\partial F$. Over some small time interval, Δt, our change in wealth can be calculated as

$$\Delta Wealth = \frac{\partial c}{\partial F}\Delta F - \Delta c. \tag{2.62}$$

Because the position is riskless, it must earn the instantaneous riskless rate r. From here, Black derives the following differential equation

$$\frac{\partial c}{\partial t} + \frac{1}{2}\frac{\partial^2 c}{\partial F^2}\sigma^2 F^2 = rc. \tag{2.63}$$

This equation is like the differential equation for an option on a security derived in equation 2.9 of Section I. There is one term missing from equation 2.63, however, as the investment in a futures contract is zero (effectively as only margin has to be posted). By applying the boundary conditions

$$c = F - X \qquad \text{if} \qquad F \geq X,$$
$$c = 0 \qquad \text{if} \qquad \text{otherwise}$$

Black derives the following formula for the value of a commodity call option:

$$c^B = e^{-r(T-t)}\left[FN\left(d_1^B\right) - XN\left(d_2^B\right)\right] \tag{2.64}$$

where

$$d_1^B = \frac{\ln\left(\frac{F}{X}\right) + \frac{\sigma^2}{2}(T-t)}{\sigma\sqrt{T-t}} \quad \text{and} \tag{2.64a}$$

$$d_2^B = \frac{\ln\left(\frac{F}{X}\right) + \frac{\sigma^2}{2}(T-t)}{\sigma\sqrt{T-t}} = d_1 - \sigma\sqrt{T-t}. \tag{2.64b}$$

The value for a commodity put option is

$$p^B = e^{-r(T-t)}\left[XN\left(-d_2^B\right) - FN\left(-d_1^B\right)\right].$$ (2.65)

The superscripts B denote Black's Futures Option Pricing Model. These formulae are the same as the value on an option paying a continuous dividend equal to the risk-free rate r. Also, the same formulas result from substituting F for S and letting $\delta = r$ in the Merton model above (the adjustments to the Merton model for pricing European options on futures contracts).

Garman-Kohlhagen

Garman and Kohlhagen (1983) derive a model to price European-style options on foreign currency. By following an analysis similar to Black and Scholes (1973), they derive what is basically an extension of the original B-S formula. Their model is

$$c^{GK} = Se^{-p(T-t)}N\left(d_1^{GK}\right) - XE^{-r(T-t)}N\left(d_2^{GK}\right)$$ (2.66)

where

$$d_1^{GK} = \frac{\ln\left(\dfrac{Se^{-p(T-t)}}{X}\right) + \left(r + \dfrac{\sigma^2}{2}\right)(T-t)}{\sigma\sqrt{T-t}} \quad \text{and}$$ (2.66a)

$$d_1^{GK} = d_1 - \sigma\sqrt{T-t}.$$ (2.66b)

Here, S is the spot exchange rate and ρ is the foreign risk-free rate.

There are three basic deficiencies with applying any of the above mentioned models to the pricing of options on indices, currencies and/or futures contracts. They are:

1. The Cost-of-Carry model does not strictly hold for all commodities. It does hold fairly well for futures on precious metals and non-interest bearing financial instruments.

2. It is unlikely that the assumptions of a constant volatility for the asset underlying the futures contract and that α is only a function of time holds for interest-bearing securities (e.g. T-bond or Eurodollar futures). This means that it is also unlikely that the futures price on such a commodity follows a process similar to that outlined in equation 2.61 above.

3. Lastly, the above models apply to European-style options whereas most futures options are of the American variety. There are generally no closed-form solutions or analytical formulas available for American-style options. This means some analytical approximation has to be used.

The following section addresses some of the literature that addresses problem two above. As for problem three above, options on futures are equivalent to options on the spot when pricing European-style options and both the futures and the options contracts have concurrent expiration dates. This is not always true for American-style options.

Consider an American call option on some commodity and an American call option on a futures contract on the same commodity. Assume both expire simultaneously and that the underlying security is a non-dividend paying security. From the analysis in Section I, it is known that the option on the underlying is worth more alive than dead and will not be exercised early. However, the option on the futures may be. This is because the option on the futures will have a greater value because the futures price will always be higher than the spot price prior to expiration (this according the Cost-of-Carry Model). The same line of reasoning can explain why an American put on a futures can be less than an otherwise equivalent American-put on spot.

The spread between American options on futures and American options on spot is reduced through the inclusion of dividends. If the dividends are large enough, it is possible for the futures price to be less than the spot price. This provides a further difficulty in pricing. Additional reasons that a discrepancy may exist between the price of options on futures versus options on spot include: (1) Non-concurrent expiration dates for the options and futures contracts; and (2) the futures contract may be more liquid than the underlying commodity thereby making options on the futures more attractive than options on spot (if you do exercise a futures option you can simply offset to get out of the position whereas with an option on spot you often must take or make delivery).

SECTION IV: INTEREST RATE DERIVATIVE SECURITIES

Many options contracts are written on interest bearing securities such as T-bonds and Eurodollars. Recall in Section I that Merton (1973) developed a model for pricing options on discount bonds. Merton defines $B(t)$ as the value of a discount bond that matures at the same time as the option and which has a payoff of \$1 at maturity. It is assumed that B follows a process similar to that of the stock as

$$\frac{dB}{B} = \mu_B dt + \sigma_B dz_B$$

where μ_B = the growth rate in the bond price, σ_B = the volatility of B, dz_B is a Wiener process, and μ_B is stochastic. Merton the follows an analysis similar to that of the B-S analysis outlined earlier in this chapter to derive the following European call price as:

$$c = SN(d_1) - BXN(d_2)$$

$$d_1 = \frac{\ln\left(\frac{S}{X}\right) - \ln B + \left(\frac{\sigma'^2}{2}\right)(T-t)}{\sigma'\sqrt{T-t}}$$

$$d_2 = d_1 - \sigma'\sqrt{T-t}$$

$$\sigma'\sqrt{T-t} = \int_t^T \left(\sigma^2 + \sigma_B^2 - 2\rho\sigma\sigma_B\right)dt$$

where σ = the stock's volatility and ρ = the instantaneous correlation between the stock and bond prices, and $B = e^{-R(T-t)}$. Here R is the rate of interest on a risk-free bond whose maturity coincides with the options expiration date. Therefore, this model is a derivation of the B-S model with R and σ' replacing r and σ. According to Hull and White (1990) one of the criticisms of this model is that the volatility of the discount bond is a known function of time. Furthermore, as pointed out in Section III above, many of the options on such securities are American-style. For a zero-coupon bond, it will never be optimal to exercise the option early (this analysis follows the reasoning as to why an American-style option on a non-dividend paying stock will not be exercised early), and an American call can be treated as a European option. If the underlying bond is of the coupon-paying type, then adjustments can be made to the basic European models that are similar to the adjustments made for dividend paying stocks. This will only net an approximation however.

In the case of an American-style futures option on an interest bearing security, it can be optimal for early exercise. As pointed out earlier, there are no solutions to such option pricing problems, and some analytical approximation must be used. This is because, with the possibility of early exercise, the practitioner must be concerned with bond price uncertainty throughout the life of the option, not just at the end of the option life as with European-style options.

Other problems include the fact that there are many different types of interest rate derivative securities such as caps, swaps, swaptions, bond options, captions, mortgage backed securities, etc. Often, different models are used to price different securities. Hull and White (1990) state that Black's (1976) model is often used with the assumption that forward interest rates are lognormal to price caps (interest rate caps provide insurance against the rate of interest on a floating rate loan rising above a certain level). Black's model is also often used to price European bond options and swaptions (a swaption gives the buyer the right to enter into a certain interest rate swap at a certain time in the future), using the assumption that forward bond prices are lognormal.

Hull and White (1990) assert that using different models in different situations poses a number of problems. The first problem is that there is no easy way of making the volatility parameters in one model consistent with those in another. The second problem is that difficulty arises in trying to aggregate exposures across different interest-rate securities. The authors use the example that it is hard to ascertain the extent to which the volatility exposure of a swaption can be offset by a position in caps. Finally, they note that it is difficult to value nonstandard securities. The remainder of this section will be used to discuss models of the term structure (Vasicek [1977], and Cox, Ingersoll, & Ross [1985b]).

Term Structure Models

Some early yield curve models assumed that short-term interest rates r, were determined by a process similar to that which determines stock prices (see equation 2.1 of Section I above). Such models ignore the tendency of mean reversion for interest rates. Mean reversion is the tendency for interest rates to gravitate toward some long term average and there are three effects related to mean reversion:

1. interest rate volatility becomes a decreasing function of maturity,

2. forward rate volatility is inversely related to forward contract maturity, and

3. bond price volatility is not necessarily proportional to a discount bond's maturity or duration.

Following this, Vasicek (1977) developed a model of short-term interest rates where r is determined by the following mean reverting process

$$dr = \alpha(b - r)dt + \sigma dw \qquad (2.67)$$

where α, b and σ are positive constants and dw is a standard Wiener process. The short-term rate, r, tends toward a long-run average rate, b, at some rate α. Vasicek defines the value of a discount bond paying \$1 at maturity at time $= t$ as

$$P(t,T) = E\left[e^{-r(T-t)}\right] \qquad (2.68)$$

where is the average short-term interest rate, r, over the interval $T - t$. Vasicek solves equation 2.68 as

$$P(t,T) = A(t,T)e^{-B(T-t)r} \qquad (2.69)$$

where

$$B(t,T) = \frac{1 - e^{-\alpha(T-t)}}{\alpha} \qquad (2.70)$$

when $\alpha \neq 0$ and

$$A(t,T) = \exp\left[\frac{\left(B(t,T) - T + t\right)\left(\alpha^2 b - \sigma^2/2\right)}{\alpha^2} - \frac{\sigma^2 B(t,T)^2}{4\alpha}\right] \qquad (2.71)$$

when $\alpha = 0$, $B(t,T) = T - t$ and $A(t,T) = exp[\sigma^2(T - t)^3/6]$. Although this model is rather rich (upward sloping, downward sloping, and humped yield curves can be derived depending on the choices for α, b, and σ), this model can lead to a negative short term interest rate r.

Cox, Ingersoll, and Ross (1985) develop an intertemporal general equilibrium asset pricing model to study the term structure of interest rates that does not lead to the possibility of a negative r. With the CIR model, short-term interest rates are determined by the process

$$dr = \alpha(b - r)dt + \sigma\sqrt{r}dw \qquad (2.72)$$

where all variables are as defined for the Vasicek model above. This is the same process as Vasicek's with the exception that the standard deviation is proportional to $\sqrt{r}$.

With the above process for short-term interest rates, CIR develop the following model for bond prices

$$P(t,T) = A(t,T)e^{-B(t,T)r} \qquad (2.73)$$

where

$$B(t,T) = \frac{2\left(e^{-B(T-t)} - 1\right)}{2\gamma + \left(\alpha + \lambda + \gamma\right)\left(e^{\gamma(T-t)} - 1\right)}, \qquad (2.74)$$

$$A(t,T) = \left[\frac{2\gamma e^{\gamma(\alpha+\lambda+\gamma)(T-t)/2}}{2\gamma + \left(\alpha + \lambda + \gamma\right)\left(e^{\gamma(T-t)} - 1\right)}\right]^{\frac{2ab}{\sigma^2}}, \qquad (2.75)$$

$$\gamma = \sqrt{\left(\alpha + \lambda\right)^2 + 2\sigma^2}, \qquad (2.76)$$

and λ is a risk premium factor.

This model is also rich in that it can be used to derive yield curves that are upward sloping, downward sloping and/or slightly humped.

CIR next derive solutions for contingent claims on discount bonds. These formulas can be used to price European call and put options on discount bonds. As with previous models however, the CIR model is not appropriate for coupon-bearing bonds or for American-style options on interest bearing securities.

Many other models have been developed to aid in the pricing of contingent claims on interest bearing securities. Ho and Lee (1986) derive an arbitrage-free interest rate movements model (AR model). They show how such a model can be used to price interest rate contingent claims relative to the complete term structure of interest rates. Their model is attractive because it provides a tractable means for pricing a broad range of securities including bond options and callable bonds. The disadvantages of the Ho and Lee model are that all spot and forward rates have the same instantaneous standard deviation and the model has no mean reversion.

Hull and White (1990) attempt to address some of the problems relating to the above interest rate derivative models by extending the Vasicek and CIR models so that: (1) they are consistent with both the current term structure of interest rates and; (2) that they are consistent with either the current volatilities of all spot interest rates or the current volatilities of all forward interest rates. The authors found that their extension of the Vasicek model was very tractable as the parameters of the process followed by the short-term interest rate and European bond option prices could be determined analytically. Unfortunately, this model, as with previous models, fails to address American option pricing.

SECTION V: INTEREST RATE FUTURES OPTIONS WITH FUTURES STYLE MARGINING

With a traditional options contract, the buyer must pay the full amount of the premium while the option writer (seller) posts margin. An alternative is for both the buyer and the writer to post margin as with a futures contract. The option value would be marked to market daily during the life of the option, and gains and losses would be paid and collected on a daily basis as with traditional futures contracts. However, a futures-style option differs from a traditional futures contract in that the owner of the option has the right to exercise the option at the options expiration if European or on any business day if American. Futures-style margining for options is currently used at the London International Financial Futures and Options Exchange (LIFFE) and the Sydney Futures Exchange. Although the use of such options has been proposed in the United States, currently no exchange uses them. The remainder of this section reviews the literature relating to the valuation of options with futures-style margining.

Lieu

Lieu (1990) was the first to apply the techniques utilized in the Black-Scholes analysis to derive put and call option pricing formulas for futures-style options. Lieu begins by stating that the traditional B-S formula is not appropriate for futures-style options, even if they are European options, because of the marking to market. Lieu assumes as Black (1976) did that futures prices are determined by the process

$$dF = \mu F dt + \sigma F dw \qquad (2.77)$$

where all variables are as defined earlier. The call price function is given *as* $c(t) = c(F(t),t)$. With futures-style margining, the value of a call option will be zero at time t. This is also the case with a futures contract. Therefore, a hedge portfolio consisting of a futures contract and a futures-style option must also have a zero value at time t. Based on these assumptions, Lieu derives the following p.d.e.:

$$\frac{1}{2} \frac{\partial^2 c}{\partial F^2} \sigma^2 F^2 + \frac{\partial c}{\partial t} = 0. \qquad (2.78)$$

By applying the boundary conditions

$$c = \max(F_T - X, 0),$$

where T is the option's expiration date, the p.d.e. in equation 2.78 can be solved. The p.d.e. in equation 2.78 can be thought of as a special case of Black's (1976) p.d.e. where $r = 0$. The price for a futures-style call option is

$$c = FN(d_1) - XN(d_2), \qquad (2.79)$$

where

$$d_1 = \frac{\ln\left(\dfrac{F}{X}\right) + \dfrac{\sigma^2}{2}(T-t)}{\sigma\sqrt{T-t}} \quad \text{and} \qquad (2.79a)$$

$$d_2 = d_1 - \sigma\sqrt{T-t}. \qquad (2.79b)$$

The value for a futures-style put option is

$$p = XN(-d_2) - FN(-d_1). \qquad (2.80)$$

The only difference between this model and Black's (1976) model is that the discount factor $e^{-r(T-t)}$ drops out of Lieu's model and interest rates drop out of the futures-style option formula. Lieu claims this has intuitive appeal as it is no longer necessary to consider borrowing to pay for an option premium, or investing premiums from short options. Unfortunately, Lieu concludes by stating that his model is not applicable to the options contracts traded at LIFFE. This is because LIFFE trades options on foreign-currency cash not futures as required by his model. LIFFE does trade options on interest rate futures, but interest rate futures contracts do not satisfy the distributional assumptions that are demanded by the Black-Scholes type option models.

Fortunately, LIFFE does trade Financial Time Stock Exchange 100 Index (FTSE) futures for which Lieu's model is applicable. Unfortunately, Lieu reports that the trading volume in FTSE at LIFFE is virtually nonexistent and trading information for this contract is not reported at all.

Lieu concludes by reiterating that the interest rate factor is completely dropped from his formula and that the early-exercise feature of American futures options no longer matters for the options with futures-style margining. Therefore, the value of European futures options and American futures options converge. He further states that futures-style margining turns an option on a futures contract into a futures contract on a stock-style option. Thus, a futures-style option can be considered more of a futures contract than an option contract.

Kuo

Kuo (1991) derives a valuation model for a futures-style option contract on futures. He begins by assuming futures prices follow the process outlined in equation 2.80 above. Where he differs from Lieu however, is with his assumption as to the value of his hedge portfolio at time t. Lieu sets that value equal to zero by assuming that the amount of margin that has to be posted by each side is trivial. Kuo does not adhere to that assumption and states that the marking to market required for futures-style options means that day-to-day contract gains/losses will have to be invested (or borrowed) at uncertain future interest rates. Kuo assumes that interest rates follow

$$dr = \alpha r dt + \sigma_r r dw, \tag{2.81}$$

where α is the drift for the interest rate and σ_2 is the instantaneous standard deviation of the interest rate. This specification is somewhat suspect however, as it is not a mean reverting process.

Using the above, Kuo derives the following p.d.e. for the value of a futures-style call option:

$$\frac{\partial c}{\partial t} + \frac{1}{2}\frac{\partial^2 c}{\partial F^2}\sigma_F^2 F^2 + \frac{1}{2}\frac{\partial^2 c}{\partial r^2}\sigma_r^2 r^2 + \sigma_F \sigma_r Fr\frac{\partial^2 c}{\partial F \partial r} - \Gamma r\frac{\partial c}{\partial r} = 0, \tag{2.82}$$

where . The solution to equation 2.82 using the boundary condition that $c = Max\ (0, F - X)$ is given as

$$c = FN(d_1)\exp-\left\{(\sigma_F/\sigma_r)\left[\Gamma - 1/2\left(\sigma_F \sigma_r - \sigma_r^2\right)\right](T - t)\right\} - XN(d_2), \tag{2.83}$$

where

$$d_1 = \frac{\ln\left(\frac{F}{X}\right) + \frac{\sigma_F}{\sigma_r}\left\{\ln\ r - \left[\Gamma + \frac{1}{2}\left(\sigma_r^2 - 3\sigma_F \sigma_r\right)\right](T - t)\right\}}{\sigma_F\sqrt{2(T - t)}}, \tag{2.83a}$$

$$d_2 = d_1 - \sigma_F \sqrt{2(T-t)}. \qquad (2.83b)$$

Kuo points out that this result is different from Lieu (1990) because Lieu incorrectly ignores the impact of marking-to-market on trader's cash flows and, thus, the interim interest rates.

Chen and Scott

Chen and Scott (1993) show that Lieu's (1990) results on futures options with futures-style margining also hold in a general equilibrium model with stochastic interest rates. This implies that Lieu's model can be applied to European and American futures-style options traded on LIFFE. Chen and Scott extend Lieu's results to interest rate futures options. The authors also modify several existing models for interest rate futures options to allow for futures-style margining.

Chen and Scott first modify Black's (1976) model for pricing Eurodollar futures options. The authors state:

> The final settlement price for ED futures is determined by taking an average of the London Interbank Offer Rate (LIBOR) on the delivery day and subtracting the rate from 100. Prior to delivery, traders calculate the futures rate, which is 100 minus the futures price. Conventional ED futures options are frequently priced by applying Black's model: the futures rate is assumed to have a lognormal distribution and the short term interest rate is assumed to be fixed.

Therefore, the authors derive the value for a ED futures call as

$$C = e^{-r(T-t)}\left[(100-K)N(-d_2) - RN(-d_1)\right], \qquad (2.84)$$

where

$$d_1 = \frac{\ln\left(\dfrac{R}{100-K}\right) + \dfrac{\sigma^2}{2}(T-t)}{\sigma\sqrt{T-t}} \quad \text{and} \qquad (2.84a)$$

$$d_2 = d_1 - \sigma\sqrt{T-t}, \qquad (2.84b)$$

and where $R(t)$ is the futures rate which is equal to $100 - f(t)$, $f(t)$ is the futures price, and K is the strike price. σ is the volatility for the futures rate. Because there is an inverse relationship between interest rates and the prices of interest bearing securities, the above futures call option is equivalent to a put option on the futures rate.

In order to derive an option valuation model for ED futures options with futures-style margining, the authors assume that the futures rate is lognormally distributed. Further, they assume that R is a geometric Brownian motion process such that $R = e^x$ and x is determined by the process: $dx = \mu(x)dt + \sigma dw$. Similar to Black-Scholes (1973), Black (1976), and Lieu (1990), the authors form a riskless hedge portfolio. This portfolio consists of a position in the futures contract and an offsetting position in the futures option. This portfolio requires a zero investment; and, in equilibrium with no risk, it should provide a zero return. The resulting p.d.e. is given as:

$$\frac{\partial C}{\partial t} + \frac{1}{2}\frac{\partial^2 C}{\partial R^2}\sigma^2 R^2 = 0. \tag{2.85}$$

The solution of the above p.d.e. subject to the boundary condition that $C = Max(0, (100 - R) - K)$ is

$$C = (100 - K)N(-d_2) - RN(-d_1), \tag{2.86}$$

where

$$d_1 = \frac{\ln\left(\frac{R}{100 - K}\right) + \frac{\sigma^2}{2}(T - t)}{\sigma\sqrt{T - t}} \quad \text{and} \tag{2.86a}$$

$$d_2 = d_1 - \sigma\sqrt{T - t}, \tag{2.86b}$$

This is similar to the model in equation 2.84 except the term $e^{-r(T-t)}$ has dropped out.

Chen and Scott next make an adjustment in their analysis because the above model does not incorporate any of the potential effects of mean reversion in short-term interest rates. They assume that LIBOR is determined by a stochastic process. They further assume that LIBOR is equal to e^y and that y is determined by the following mean reverting diffusion process:

$$dy = \alpha(b - y)dt + \sigma dw \qquad (2.87)$$

where α is the rate of adjustment and b is the long run average, and α, b, and σ are all greater than zero. They let the risk premium on y equal $\lambda\sigma^2$. The authors derive the p.d.e. for a zero investment hedged portfolio as

$$\frac{\partial C}{\partial t} + \frac{1}{2}\frac{\partial^2 C}{\partial R^2}\sigma^2 R^2 e^{-2\alpha(T_f - t)} = 0. \qquad (2.88)$$

The solution of this p.d.e. is given as

$$d_1 = \frac{\ln\left(\frac{R}{100 - K}\right) + \frac{1}{2}V}{\sqrt{V}}, \text{ and} \qquad (2.88a)$$

$$d_2 = d_1 - \sqrt{V}, \qquad (2.88b)$$

and where

$$V = \frac{\sigma^2}{2\alpha}e^{-2\alpha(T_f - t)}(1 - e)^{-2\alpha(T - t)}. \qquad (2.88c)$$

With the above model, options with longer maturities will have lower average volatilities due to the mean reversion.

Recall from Section IV, a CIR one factor model of the term structure was assumed to be determined by the process

$$dr = \alpha(b - r)dt + \sigma\sqrt{r}dw,$$

and that CIR (1985) derived the price of a discount bond that pay \$1 at maturity as

$$P(t,T) = A(t,T)e^{-B(t,T)r}$$

where

$$B(t,T) = \frac{2\left(e^{\gamma(T-t)} - 1\right)}{2\gamma + (\alpha + \lambda + \gamma)\left(e^{\gamma(T-t)} - 1\right)},$$

$$A(t,T) = \left[\frac{2\gamma e^{(\alpha+\lambda+\gamma)(T-t)/2}}{2\gamma + (\alpha + \lambda + \gamma)\left(e^{\gamma(T-t)} - 1\right)}\right]^{\frac{2ab}{\sigma^2}},$$

$$\gamma = \sqrt{(\alpha + \lambda)^2 + 2\sigma^2},$$

and λr is a risk premium for the interest rate. Using this result, Chen and Scott show that the price of a futures contract on the discount bond is determined as

$$f(r, t; T_f, s) = 100 A^*(t, T_f, s) e^{-B^*(t, T_f, s)r} \qquad (2.89)$$

where

$$A^*(t, T_f, s) = A(T_f, s) \left(\frac{2(\alpha + \lambda)}{2(\alpha + \lambda) + \sigma^2 B(T_f, s)\left(1 - e^{-(\alpha+\lambda)(T_f - t)}\right)}\right)^{\frac{2ab}{\sigma^2}}, \quad (2.89a)$$

and

$$B^*(t, T_f, s) = \left(\frac{2(\alpha + \lambda)e^{-(\alpha+\lambda)(T_f - t)} B(T_f, s)}{2(\alpha + \lambda) + \sigma^2 B(T_f, s)\left(1 - e^{-(\alpha+\lambda)(T_f - t)}\right)}\right). \qquad (2.89b)$$

The authors next derive the following p.d.e. by setting up a zero investment hedged portfolio of the futures and the futures option as:

$$\frac{\partial C}{\partial t} + \frac{1}{2}\frac{\partial^2 C}{\partial r^2}\sigma^2 r^2 \frac{\partial C}{\partial r}\left(\alpha b - \alpha r - \lambda r\right) = 0. \tag{2.90}$$

The solution for this p.d.e. is given as:

$$C = f\left(r,t;T_f,s\right)\chi^2\left(z_1;\frac{4\alpha b}{\sigma^2},\lambda_1^*\right) - K\chi^2\left(z_2;\frac{4\alpha b}{\sigma^2},\lambda_2^*\right), \tag{2.91}$$

where $\chi^2(z{:}v,\ \lambda*)$ is the non-central chi-square distribution function with degrees of freedom, v, and non-centrality parameter, λ^*, and

$$z_2 = \frac{4(\alpha+\lambda)r^*}{\sigma^2\left(1-e^{-(\alpha+\lambda)(T-t)}\right)}, \tag{2.91a}$$

$$\lambda_2^* = \frac{4(\alpha+\lambda)re^{-(\alpha+\lambda)(T-t)}}{\sigma^2\left(1-e^{-(\alpha+\lambda)(T-t)}\right)}, \tag{2.91b}$$

$$z_1 = z_2 + 2B^*\left(T,T_f,s\right)r^*, \tag{2.91c}$$

$$\lambda_1^* = \frac{2(\alpha+\lambda)\lambda_2^*}{2(\alpha+\lambda)+\sigma^2 B^*\left(T,T_f,s\right)\left(1-e^{-(\alpha+\lambda)(T-t)}\right)}, \tag{2.91d}$$

$$r^* = \frac{1}{B^*\left(T,T_f,s\right)}\ln\left(\frac{100A^*\left(T,T_f,s\right)}{K}\right). \tag{2.91e}$$

Although this is a complex model, all of the above models are simplified for pricing interest rate futures options with futures-style margining because there is no discount factor in the solutions. Chen and Scott also conclude that the most useful result of their analysis is that futures options with futures-style margining should not be exercised early because their prices should exceed the intrinsic value prior to expiration. This leads to the conclusion that American futures options will have the same prices as comparable European futures options, and one can price the American futures options with a European pricing model.

Chen and Scott's analysis has two shortcomings. The first is that all of the above adjustments ignore the impact of marking-to-market on traders' cash flows. Secondly, these models are applicable only for futures-style options on non-coupon bearing securities. While this second short-coming is not a problem for options on T-bills, Eurodollars, and other non-coupon bearing securities, it does limit the model's scope.

SECTION VI: EMPIRICAL STUDIES

MacBeth and Merville

MacBeth and Merville (1979) assume that the B-S model correctly prices at-the-money options and uses the B-S formula to compute implied volatilities. The implied volatility is found by setting the B-S option price equal to the market price for at-the-money options ($S = X$) and solving for the volatility, σ. Based on their assumptions about how the B-S model priced at-the-money options and on the volatility assumption, MacBeth and Merville examined how well the B-S model priced in-the-money and out-of-the-money options. Their results indicated the presence of pricing biases. The first bias was that the B-S model tended to underprice in-the-money options and overprice out-of-the-money options. The second finding was that the pricing bias was positively related to how far the option was in-the-money or out-of-the-money. For example, consider two options on the same stock, identical in every way except for strike price. Suppose the stock price is $25, and that call option A has a strike of $22.50 and that call B has a strike of $20.00. Both would be underpriced by the B-S model, but call B would tend to be more seriously underpriced than option A. Similarly, an option that was more out-of-the-money than an otherwise identical option would tend to be more overpriced by the B-S model. The authors also found that the underpricing/overpricing effect tended to decrease as the time until maturity decreased. This indicates that the B-S model may seriously misprice options that have a long time until maturity and that are deep in-the-money or deep out-of-the-money.

In another study, MacBeth and Merville (1980) compared the B-S model to a constant elasticity of variance (CEV) model developed by Cox and Ross (1976). While the B-S model assumes that the volatility is constant, the CEV model assumes that volatility changes when the stock price changes. When a stock price declines, it is assumed that operating performance has declined; and because the firm's fixed costs remain constant, the stock's volatility has increased. The opposite is true for a stock price increase which leads to a decrease in volatility. MacBeth and Merville found that the CEV model provided better performance than the B-S model.

Rubinstein

Rubinstein (1985) compared the basic Black-Scholes model with several option pricing extensions, including the constant elasticity of variance (CEV) model, Geske's compound option pricing model, a pure jump model and a jump-diffusion model. The author conducted non-parametric tests on options which differed only in terms of exercise price or time to maturity covering a time period of August 21, 1976, to August 31, 1978. Rubinstein subdivided his time interval into two sub-periods covering August 21, 1976, through October 21, 1977, and October 24, 1977, through August 31, 1978. For the first sub-period, his findings were consistent with those of MacBeth and Merville (1979) above in that the B-S model tended to underprice in-the-money options and overprice out-of-the-money options. This pricing bias reversed itself in the second sub-period, however. In the second sub-period, the B-S model tended to overprice in-the-money options and underprice out-of-the-money options. Although some of the alternative models are better suited to handle certain pricing biases resulting from the B-S model, none of the alternative models could handle the bias switch over the two sub-periods; and therefore, none of the alternative models were found to be superior to the B-S model over both sub-periods.

Geske and Roll

Geske and Roll (1984) review much of the empirical evidence on the pricing biases produced by the B-S formula when used to price American call options, in particular the biases related to the exercise price, the time to maturity, and the variance. The authors point out that when using Black's ad hoc adjustment of the European B-S model, the pseudo-American call value will be less than the actual American value because the pseudo method does not fully reflect the opportunities available to the American call holder. The true American call value incorporates the conditional probability of exercising prematurely at each ex-dividend date, as opposed to certain early exercise or no exercise. The authors illustrate that inappropriate treatment of dividends leads to inaccurate estimates as to the probability of early exercise which in turn can produce the striking price, time-to-expiration, and variance biases reported above.

Geske and Roll demonstrate that the original and reverse striking price biases reported by MacBeth and Merville (1979) and by Rubinstein (1985)[4] can be explained by the early exercise phenomenon. The authors point out that although the B-S misspricing is most noticeable for in- and out-of-the-money options, the pseudo-American B-S model will underprice all dividend-paying American options, including at-the-moneys. The results also indicate that the pseudo-American method will present an underpricing of near-maturity American call options. Finally, the authors report that the variance bias could be attributed to nonstationary stock volatility which could be induced by dividend uncertainty.

Hull and White

One of the assumptions underlying the B-S model is that the underlying asset's variance is constant (constant volatility). In practice, however, it is often common to adjust the volatility frequently when pricing options. Hull and White (1987 and 1988) develop models to account for the possibility of stochastic volatility. Hull and White (1987) show that if the volatility is uncorrelated with the stock price then the appropriate option value is the B-S value integrated over the distribution of the average variance rate during the life of the option as follows:

$$c_{HW} = \int c_{BS}(\bar{V}) g(\bar{V}) d\bar{V} \qquad (2.92)$$

where c_{BS} = the Black-Scholes price, $\bar{V}$ = the average value of the variance σ^2, and g is the probability density function of $\bar{V}$. Their analysis indicates that the B-S model produces systematic pricing biases. In general, the B-S model overprices options that are at-the-money or close-to-the-money while underpricing options that are deep in or deep out-of-the-money.

In a related study, Hull and White (1987) examined the case where stock price and volatility are instantaneously correlated. They find that when there is a positive correlation the B-S model tends to underprice out-of-the-money calls and overprice out-of-the-money puts. The authors posit that this occurs because when the stock price increases, volatility has a tendency to increase. So, if we are assuming stock prices follow a geometric Brownian motion, as does the B-S model, there will be a greater likelihood of very high stock prices. With low stock prices, volatility decreases, decreasing the likelihood of very low stock prices under geometric Brownian motion.

For the situation where stock price and volatility are negatively correlated, the B-S model tends to overprice out-of-the-money calls and underprice out-of-the-money puts. Here, a large stock price leads to a lower volatility thereby decreasing the likelihood of very high stock prices. With a low stock price, volatility increases, increasing the likelihood of very low stock prices.

Hull and White report that the pricing biases caused by stochastic volatility are not very large in absolute terms for options with less than one year to expiration. However, they report that in percentage terms, the biases found can be large for deep-out-of-the-money options and that these biases are positively related with time until expiration.

Shastri and Tandon

As has been discussed, in general, European option pricing models are not applicable for pricing American-style options. Shastri and Tandon (1986) examine the pricing accuracy of the European and American models for options on futures. In their study, they utilize the European futures option pricing model of Black (1976) and a modified version of the Geske and Johnson (1984) analytic valuation formula for American options.

Their results indicate that the European model can be used to price American options on futures contracts if the option is not deep in the money and is near maturity. Furthermore, the European model performed well when applied to options whose underlying futures contract has low volatility. In cases where the risk-free rate was high, the American model provided superior performance. Their results indicate that, although there are instances where a European model can be used to approximate American futures options prices, situations still exist that require an analytical approximation of such options.

SUMMARY

In summary, the basic B-S analysis above has several limitations. The B-S formula is for European options that do not pay dividends only. In reality, most stocks pay dividends and many options are of the American variety (i.e. they can be exercised prior to the expiration date). If a stock is viewed as option on the value of the firm, then an option on that stock is really an option on an option (also known as a compound option). It may be possible that the above mentioned pricing biases are due to the fact that the B-S model does not price compound options very well. The B-S analysis also assumes that the underlying stock price follows a continuous time path. Furthermore, the assumptions of a constant risk-free rate and constant volatility may have serious implications for the model. The incorrect specification of either of these assumptions will lead to option pricing biases. If volatilities are stochastic, rather than fixed, the B-S leads to pricing biases. Generally, when volatility is stochastic, explicit solutions for option prices do not exist and must be estimated using numerical methods. All of these issues have been addressed (although all have not been solved) by various authors. In order to address the issue of pricing American options, the B-S model has been modified, the BOPM has been utilized, and a number of approximation techniques have been proposed such as the BAW model.

As reported by Copeland and Weston (1989), there are statistically significant (if not economically significant once transactions costs are considered) biases in the B-S model and therefore, some other model may be able to provide superior performance. Hull (1993, p. 447) states that "possibly macroeconomic variables affect option prices in a way that is as yet not fully understood." This would indicate the need for an option pricing model that was able to include macroeconomic variables. Furthermore, B-S models assume the underlying asset's value is lognormally distributed. According to Hull (1993, p. 449):

> If the right tail of the true distribution is fatter than the right tail of the lognormal distribution, there will be a tendency for the Black-Scholes models to underprice out-of-the-money calls and in-the-money puts[5].

If the left tail of the true distribution is fatter than the left tail of the lognormal distribution, there will be a tendency for the Black-Scholes models to underprice out-of-the-money puts and in-the-money calls. When either tail is too thin relative to the lognormal distribution, the opposite biases are observed.

When other types of options are considered (e.g. futures style options and options on interest bearing securities), the basic B-S model becomes inadequate. Furthermore, none of the approximation techniques developed apply uniformly to the many different types of options, and some of these techniques only apply for options with certain expirations. The binding theme in the above studies is that although the B-S model and its extensions can provide good performance, biases still exist and so a more comprehensive and more flexible model needs to be developed to address these issues.

NOTES

1. A Wiener process is a particular kind of stochastic process that has been utilized in the field of finance to model stock price behavior. For a description of a standard Wiener process, consult any derivative securities textbook, such as John Hull's *Options, Futures and Other Derivative Securities*, Prentice Hall, 1993.

2. A discussion of Ito's Lemma is beyond the scope of this text. Suffice it to say that Ito's Lemma in its simplest form is the fundamental theorem of stochastic calculus and that further discussion for the initiated can be found in a stochastic calculus textbook or an advanced derivative securities text.

3. Named for French mathematician Siméon-Denis Poisson, a Poisson process is one that refers to the number of successes expected during a time interval. The criteria for a Poisson process are: (a) The occurrences of the events must be independent, (b) the probability of a single occurrence happening in a small unit of time must be proportional to the size of the unit, and (c) the probability of two or more occurrences at the same point in time is zero.

4. Geske and Roll actually quote Rubinstein's 1981 working paper which was later published in 1985 in the *Journal of Finance*.

5. For the Chen and Scott (1993) model, reverse the terms call and put in Hull's statements.

CHAPTER III

Methodology and Data

In this chapter, the data sets and methodologies utilized in this study are outlined. The chapter is divided into three sections. The first section describes how data was generated using a known Option Pricing Model (OPM) for the purpose of testing the Neural Network in a controlled environment. The second section provides a description of the real data and variables that were provided by the London International Financial Futures and Options Exchange (LIFFE) for this research. Also provided in this section is a description of the Option on Three Month Eurodollar Interest Rate Futures contract and the Three Month Eurodollar Interest Rate Future Contract. The third, and final section, provides a description of neural networks in general, their use in the field of finance and of the Genetic Adaptive Neural Network (GANN) utilized in this study.

SECTION I: SIMULATION DATA SET

In order to use the GANN in a controlled environment, call and put option prices were generated using a variation of the Black-Scholes OPM. The variation of the Black-Scholes model that was used to generate option prices was developed by Chen & Scott (1993), and requires four inputs: a futures rate, $R(t)$; a strike price, K; a volatility, σ; and time to maturity, $(T - t)$. For this simulation, the inputs $R(t)$ and σ were generated using a mean-reverting process. Nine strike prices were chosen, ranging from 93.00 to 97.00 in steps of .50, and nine maturities were chosen, ranging from 30 days to 270 days in increments of 30 days.

Description of Simulation Procedure

Eurodollar futures contracts settlement prices are quoted as a percent of the value of the underlying commodity. For Eurodollar futures, the contract size is $1,000,000. If we define $f(t)$ as the futures price, then $R(t) = 100 - f(t)$, where $R(t)$ is the futures rate. So, if we have a futures settle of 94.50, this represents 94.50% of the contract amount (or $945,000), and the futures rate is 5.5%. The first step in the simulation process was to assume this futures rate is determined by the mean-reverting process

$$dR = \kappa(\theta - R)dt + \varsigma R^\gamma \, dW \qquad (3.1)$$

where κ is the speed of adjustment parameter, θ is the long run mean, γ is an arbitrary parameter, is the instantaneous standard deviation of the futures rate, and dW is a standard Wiener process[1]. This process is referred to as the Ornstein-Uhlerbach process when $\gamma = 1$. Cox, Ingersoll, and Ross provide a detailed description of this process when $\gamma = 0.5$. The discrete time version of this process is

$$\Delta R = \kappa(\theta - R)\Delta t + \varsigma R^\gamma \, \varepsilon \sqrt{\Delta t}. \qquad (3.2)$$

For this study, the parameters for the above process were set to the following values: $\kappa = 0.1$; $\gamma = 5$; $\varsigma = 0.5$; and = 0.10. The time interval, Δt, was set at 1 day (or $1/365 = 0.00274$), and the starting futures rate was set at 3.3%. In equation 3.2, ε is a random variable chosen from a standardized normal distribution $\varepsilon \sim$i.i.d. N(0,1)). By sampling repeatedly from a standardized normal distribution and applying these values to equation 3.2, 500 futures rates were generated. The rates generated by this process are illustrated in Figure 3.1.

Although most Black-Scholes type OPMs assume a constant volatility, in practice volatilities change and are updated regularly by practitioners. For this reason (and to provide the GANN with a diverse set of inputs), 500 volatilities were generated using a process similar to that used to generate the futures rates. The mean-reverting process used to generate the volatilities is given as:

$$d\sigma = \kappa(\mu - \sigma)dt + \omega \sigma^\gamma \, dW \qquad (3.3)$$

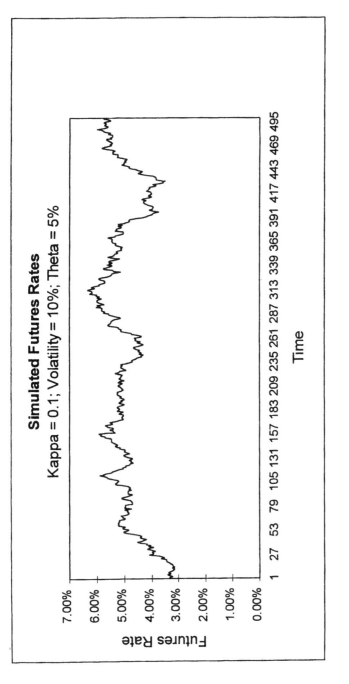

Figure 3.1 Reprinted by permission of the *Journal of Computational Intelligence in Finance*, March/April 1998, © 1998, Finance and Technology Publishing.

where μ is the average long run volatility, ω is the instantaneous standard deviation of the volatility, and all other parameters are as previously defined[2]. To generate the volatilities the parameters were set as: $\kappa = 0.1$; $\mu = 20.4$; $\gamma = 1.$; and $\omega = 0.10$. The starting σ was set at 22%. The volatilities generated by this process are illustrated in Figure 3.2. Note that the paths in both figures are dependent on the pseudo random sample generated for the parameter ε. Drawing more sets of random variables from a standardized normal distribution would yield different paths.

The next step in the simulation process involved choosing values for the inputs K and τ (where $\tau = T - t$). Strike prices of 93.00 through 97.00 in steps of .50 were chosen, yielding nine possible strike prices. Maturities of 30 days through 270 days were chosen, in steps of 30 days, yielding nine possible maturities. This meant a total of 40,500 (500 futures rates and volatilities entered simultaneously times 9 possible strike prices times 9 possible maturities) calls and puts could be generated. The final step was to calculate the call option prices using

$$C(R,t) = (100 - K)N(-d_2) - RN(-d_1),   \tag{3.4}$$

where

$$d_1 = \frac{\ln\left(\dfrac{R}{100 - K}\right) + \dfrac{1}{2}\sigma^2\tau}{\sigma\sqrt{\tau}},   \tag{3.4a}$$

$$d_2 = d_1 - \sigma\sqrt{\tau},   \tag{3.4b}$$

and put option prices were generated using

$$P(R,t) = RN(d_1) - (100 - K)N(d_2).   \tag{3.5}$$

The variables d_1 and d_2 are the same for equation 3.5 as for equation 3.4, and $N()$ is the standard normal distribution function. This model was developed by Chen and Scott (1993) and requires some explanation[3]. The formulas at first appear reversed (the call formula resembles a standard B-S OPM put formula, and vice-versa). This

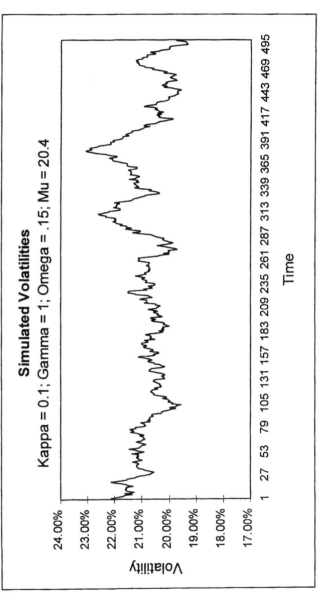

Figure 3.2 Reprinted by permission of the *Journal of Computational Intelligence in Finance*, March/April 1998, © 1998, Finance and Technology Publishing.

apparent discrepancy is explained by considering the inverse relationship between interest rates and asset prices. In this study we are examining futures-style options on 3-month Eurodollar futures contracts. The underlying asset for the option is the 3-month Eurodollar futures contract. The underlying asset for the futures contract is the Eurodollar contract with a three month maturity. This contract is a non-transferable time deposit in a commercial bank that earns a rate of interest (the 3-month London Interbank Offer Rate (LIBOR)). Therefore, the 3-month Eurodollar Futures contract is really a futures contract on an interest rate. When Eurodollar rates go up, the value of a futures contract on Eurodollars must therefore go down. A call option on a futures contract gives the buyer the right but not the obligation to take a long position in the futures (betting on an increase in futures prices) while a put option gives the buyer the right but not the obligation to take a short position in the futures contract (betting on a decline in futures prices). If the futures rate declines, the futures price increases. Thus, a futures call option is equivalent to a put on the futures rate. A futures put is equivalent to a call on the futures rate.

Descriptive Statistics for Simulation Data

The simulation process outlined above generated 40,500 observations. Descriptive statistics for the simulated data set are provided in Table 3.1. Distributions for the variables $R(t)$, σ, $C(R,t)$, and $P(R,t)$ from Table 3.1 can be viewed in Figures 3.3 through 3.6.

Observations were randomly selected from the simulation data set to create two subsets of data. To select the data subsets, random numbers were assigned to the 40,500 observations in the simulation data set. All observations with a random number less than .10 were selected for the data set that would be used to train the GANN. This netted 4,000 observations for the simulation training set. The remaining 36,500 observations were utilized as a validation data set. Due to rounding beyond 14 decimal places, some of the simulated call and put values were negative. Instead of "forcing" these values to zero, they were dropped from the data sets. This netted 3991 observations for the training data set and 36,412 observations for the holdout data set. Descriptive statistics for these two data sets are provided in Table 3.2.

Frequency distributions for the variables $R(t)$, σ, $C(R,t)$, and $P(R,t)$

Table 3.1: Descriptive Statistics for Simulation Data Set

Number of Observations: 40,500

	Mean	Standard Deviation	Skewness	Kurtosis	Minimum	Maximum
$R(t)$	4.964	0.672	-0.721	0.080	3.139	6.316
σ	0.209	0.007	0.509	0.230	0.193	0.231
τ	0.411	0.212	0.000	-1.230	0.082	0.740
Maturity*	150	77.461	0.000	-1.230	30	270
K	95.00	1.291	0.000	-1.230	93.00	97.00
$C(R,t)$	0.678	0.832	1.256	0.849	0.000	3.861
$P(R,t)$	0.642	0.782	1.130	0.140	0.000	3.316

Source: Reprinted by permission of the *Journal of Computational Intelligence in Finance*, March/April 1998, © 1998, Finance and Technology Publishing.

$R(t)$ is defined as the futures rate (100 minus the futures price), σ as the volatility of the underlying security, τ as the time to maturity (stated as a fraction of a year), K as the strike price, $C(R,t)$ as the simulated call option price and $P(R,t)$ as the simulated put option price.

* Maturity stated in number of days.

for both simulation subsets can be viewed in Figures 3.7 through 3.14. These graphs are paired for easy comparison (i.e. the C(R,t) frequency distributions for the training data set and the holdout data set are shown in successive order).

Analysis of Simulation Inputs

The call option pricing model used in the above simulation can be expressed as $C(R,t) = C(R,K,\sigma,\tau)$. The partial effects for this relationship are:

$$\frac{\partial C}{\partial R} < 0; \quad \frac{\partial C}{\partial K} < 0; \quad \frac{\partial C}{\partial \sigma} > 0; \quad \frac{\partial C}{\partial \tau} > 0.$$

These partials indicate an indirect relationship between the futures rate and the value of a call. As the futures rate declines, the value of the call option must increase, other things equal. This is because as the futures rate declines, the futures price, $(f(t))$ increases, thereby leading to an increase in the value of a call option written on that futures contract. The relationship between the futures rate and call prices is shown in Figure 3.15.

There is an indirect relationship between the exercise price, K, and the value of the call. A large exercise (strike) price means that the futures price must rise significantly (futures rate must fall significantly) to be in-the-money. Therefore, a large exercise price corresponds to a small call value. The relationship between both call and put prices and strike price is shown in Figure 3.16.

There is a direct relationship between the price of the call and the futures' volatility, σ. With a larger volatility the probability of a higher futures price (lower futures rate) is greater and so is the value of the call.

The same argument holds for the time to maturity. When τ is large, there is a greater probability of a larger futures price and, therefore, a larger call price.

The relationship for put options can also be expressed in a simplified form as $P(R,t) = P(R,K,\sigma,\tau)$ with the following partials:

$$\frac{\partial P}{\partial R} < 0; \quad \frac{\partial P}{\partial K} < 0; \quad \frac{\partial P}{\partial \sigma} > 0; \quad \frac{\partial P}{\partial \tau} > 0.$$

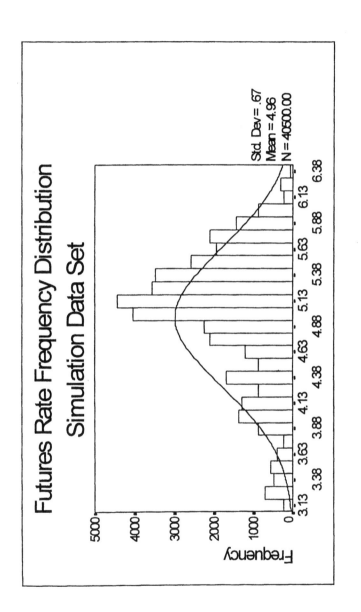

Figure 3.3

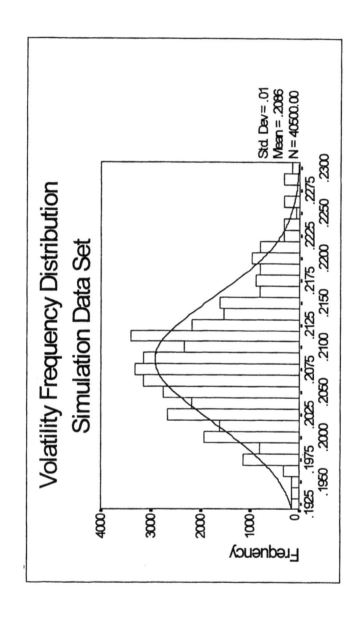

Figure 3.4

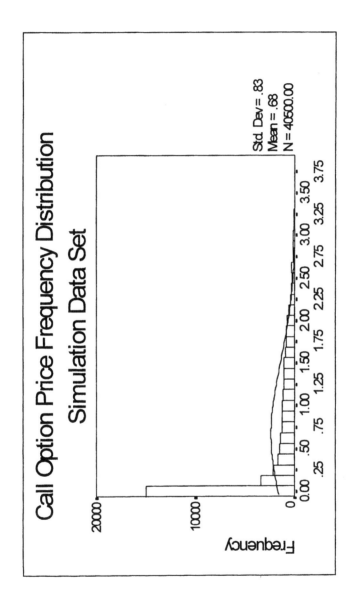

Figure 3.5

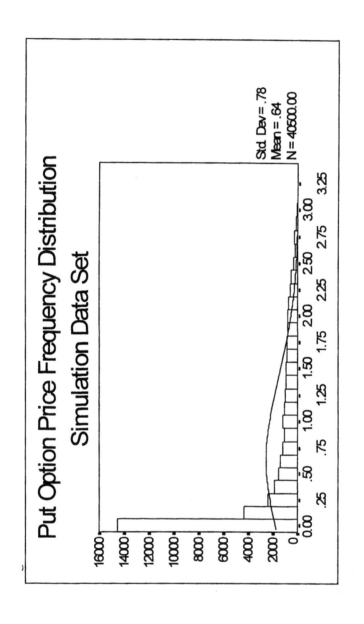

Put Option Price Frequency Distribution
Simulation Data Set

Std Dev = .78
Mean = .64
N = 40500.00

Figure 3.6

Table 3.2: Descriptive Statistics for Simulation Training Data Set

Number of Observations: 3,991

	Mean	Standard Deviation	Skewness	Kurtosis	Minimum	Maximum
$R(t)$	4.967	0.671	-0.735	0.130	3.139	6.316
σ	0.209	0.007	0.544	0.222	0.193	0.231
τ	0.411	0.211	-0.003	-1.223	0.082	0.740
Maturity*	149.925	77.131	-0.003	-1.223	30	270
K	95.00	1.306	0.009	-1.243	93.00	97.00
$C(R,t)$	0.676	0.826	1.216	0.689	0.000	3.861
$P(R,t)$	0.643	0.787	1.153	0.206	0.000	3.316

Table 3.2 (continued)

Number of Observations: 36,412

	Mean	Standard Deviation	Skewness	Kurtosis	Minimum	Maximum
$R(t)$	4.964	0.670	-0.721	0.086	3.139	6.316
σ	0.209	0.007	0.505	0.240	0.193	0.231
τ	0.412	0.212	-0.002	-1.224	0.082	0.740
Maturity*	145.493	80.029	0.105	-1.279	30	270
K	94.998	1.286	0.000	-1.222	93.00	97.00
$C(R,t)$	0.678	0.830	1.261	0.881	0.000	3.861
$P(R,t)$	0.640	0.778	1.131	0.149	0.000	3.316

Source: Reprinted by permission of the *Journal of Computational Intelligence in Finance*, March/April 1998, © 1998, Finance and Technology Publishing.

$R(t)$ is defined as the futures rate (100 minus the futures price), σ as the volatility of the underlying security, τ as the time to maturity (stated as a fraction of a year), K as the strike price, $C(R,t)$ as the simulated call option price and $P(R,t)$ as the simulated put option price.

* Maturity stated in number of days.

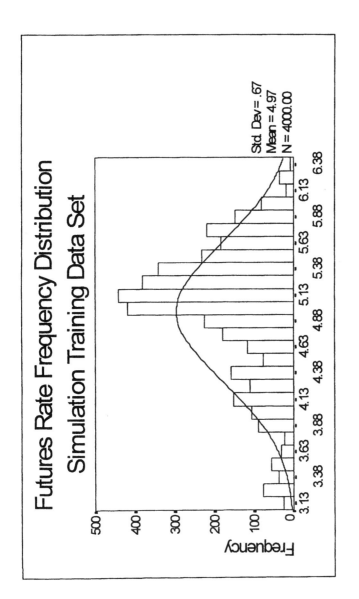

Figure 3.7

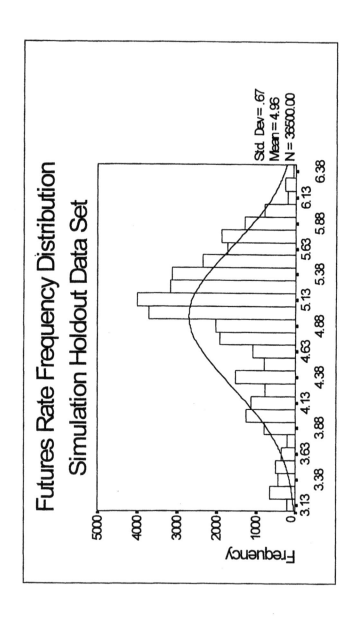

Figure 3.8

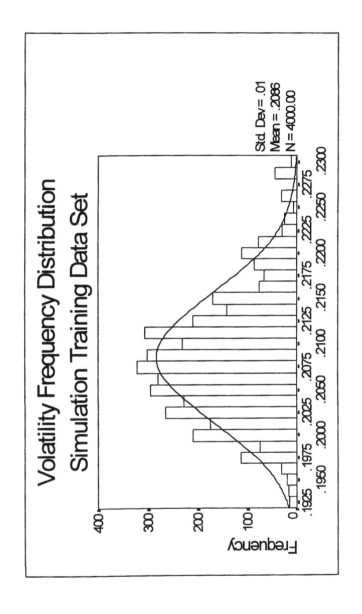

Figure 3.9

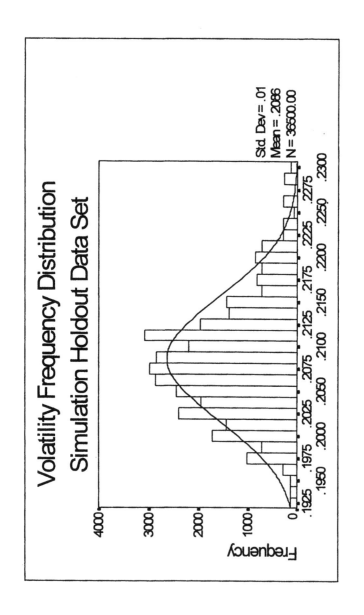

Figure 3.10

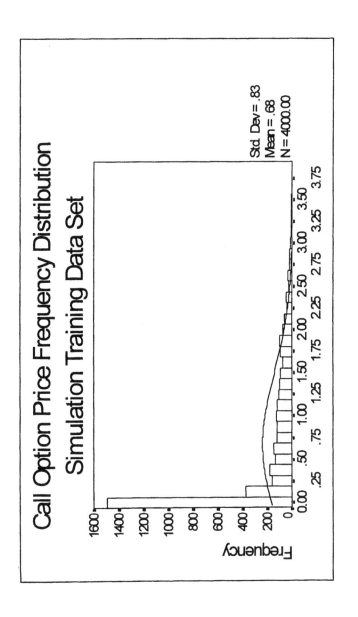

Figure 3.11

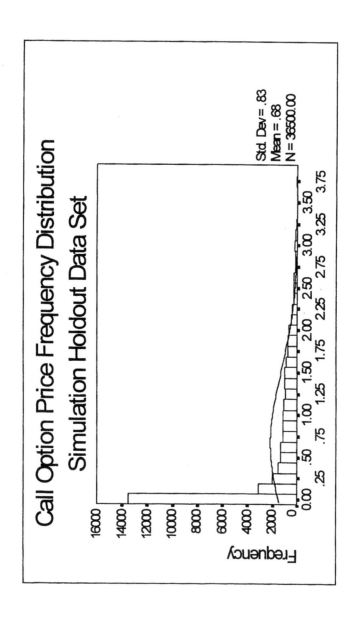

Figure 3.12

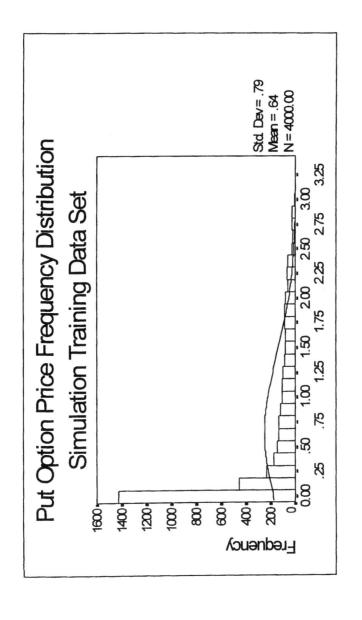

Figure 3.13

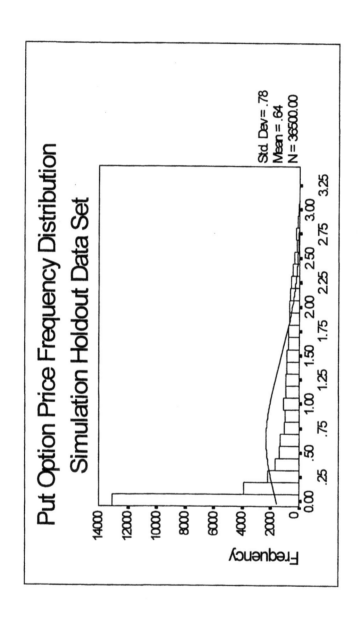

Figure 3.14

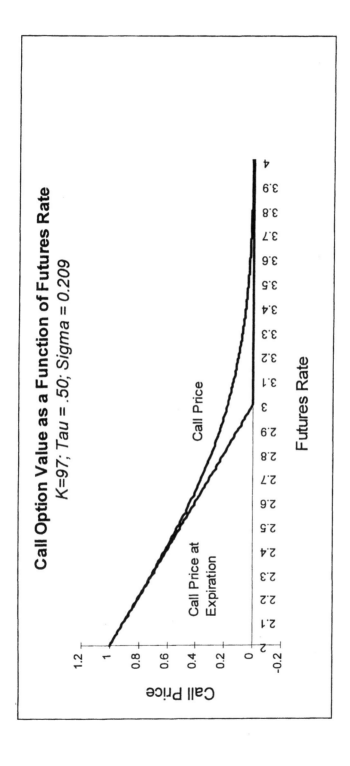

Figure 3.15

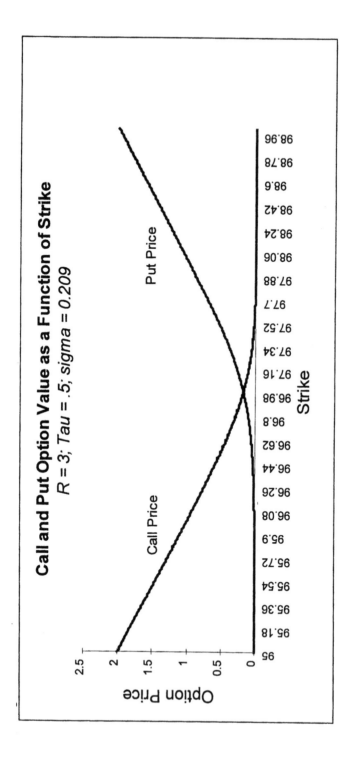

Figure 3.16

Recalling that a put option on a futures gives the buyer the right to sell the underlying security (take a short position in the futures market) at a pre-specified price and time leads to the following intuitive explanation of the above partials. When the futures rate, $R(t)$, rises, the futures price, $f(t)$, falls. The owner of a put option on such a futures contract, could exercise the option, which would give a short position in the futures market, and then offset by taking a long position on the same contract at the going market rate. Basically you sell a futures contract at the higher options strike price and simultaneously buy a futures at the lower market price, locking in a profit in the process. Therefore, the value of a put option must be inversely related to the price of the underlying futures contract and directly related to the futures rate. Figure 3.17 shows the relationship between the futures rate and a put option's value.

A large exercise price, K, increases the likelihood that the market price of the futures will be below the exercise price so the put's value must be directly related to the exercise price. This relationship was shown in Figure 3.16. With respect with time to expiration, τ, a longer time to expiration gives the put more time to increase in value which would indicate a positive relationship. However, a European put can only be exercised at expiration, so the buyer has longer to wait before he can get the exercise price. This would indicate a negative relationship between European put values and time to expiration. According to Chance (1992), the time value effect tends to dominate, meaning that puts with a longer time to expiration will have a larger value. For the simulation data set, this relationship is a positive one. The relationship between a put option's value and time to maturity for an at-the-money put can be viewed in Figure 3.18 The relationship for an in-the-money put is shown in Figure 3.19.

The relationships are the same for an at-the-money call as for an at-the-money put. As shown, the put's price increases at a decreasing rate with respect to time. For an in-the-money put (as well as for an in-the-money call, out-of-the-money put, and out-of-the-money call), the option price increases at an increasing rate with respect to time. The graph can be a little deceiving, however. Notice the vertical axis for Figure 3.19. Although the option value is increasing at an increasing rate, the scale is so small such a price change is not noticeable until τ reaches .75 (a maturity of approximately 270 days).

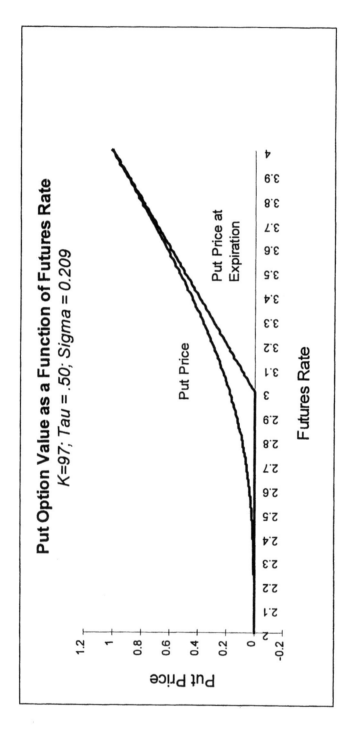

Figure 3.17

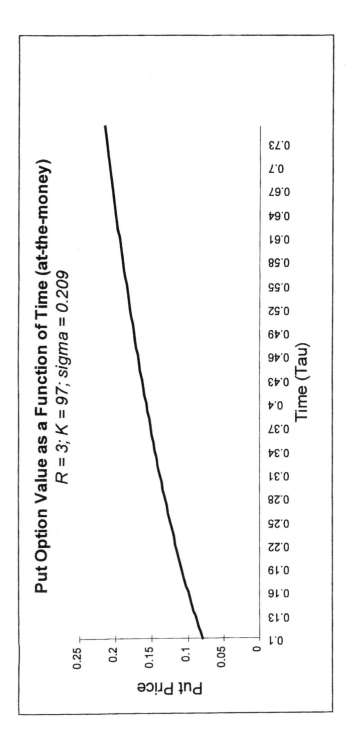

Figure 3.18

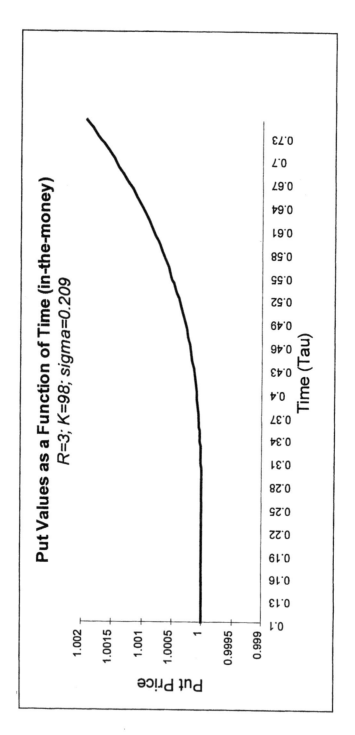

Figure 3.19

An increase in volatility, σ will affect a put in the same way as a call. A larger volatility means a larger range of prices which increases the probability that the futures' price will be below the exercise price at expiration, thereby increasing the value of the put.

SECTION II: REAL DATA

In the United States, interest rate futures contracts were introduced in 1976 and trade on the Chicago Board of Trade (CBOT), and the International Monetary Market (IMM) of the Chicago Mercantile Exchange (CME). These contracts are written on a large number of underlying securities including Treasury Bonds, Treasury Notes, Treasury Bills, 30-day Federal Funds, the Muni Bond Index and Eurodollars. Of the short-term interest rate futures contracts, the Eurodollar is the most popular and is traded on the IMM and the London International Financial Futures and Options Exchange (LIFFE). A Eurodollar is a dollar deposited in a foreign bank or a U.S. bank branch located outside the U.S. The deposit is denominated in dollars and not the currency of the country in which the bank is located. The largest Eurodollar deposit market is in London, so the Eurodollar interest rate is usually based on the London Interbank Offer Rate (LIBOR). Because the underlying security is a non-transferable time deposit in a bank, Eurodollar futures contracts are fulfilled by cash settlement rather than actual delivery of the underlying good. Futures options on 3-month Eurodollar futures contracts are traded on LIFFE. Other options on short-term interest rate futures available on LIFFE include the 3-month Sterling, 3-Month Euromark and the 3-Month Euroswiss. Options on long-term bonds are also available on LIFFE. These include options on the Long Gilt, the German Government Bond (Bund), and the Italian Government Bond.

Description of 3-Month Eurodollar Futures Option on LIFFE

Data on the 3-month Eurodollar futures and the option on 3-month Eurodollar futures for this research were provided by the LIFFE. Currently, the only exchange that trades options with futures style margining is the LIFFE. The underlying security on the 3-month Eurodollar interest rate futures option is one 3-month Eurodollar futures contract, with a contract size of $1 million. Delivery months for the futures are March, June, September, and December; and the delivery day is the first business day after the last trading day. In turn, the last trading day is two business days prior to the third Wednesday of the delivery month. Cash settlement is based on the Exchange Delivery Settlement Price (EDSP). The EDSP is based on the British Bankers' Association Interest Settlement Rate (BBAISR) for 3-month Eurodollar deposits at 11:00 am on the last trading day. The settlement price is 100 minus the BBAISR. The minimum size price movement is 0.01 which equates to $25.00[4].

The futures option is American style and can be exercised on any business day prior to 5:00 p.m. Delivery must be made on the first business day after the exercise day. Expiration occurs at 12:30 p.m. on the last trading day. The last trading day for the futures option is the last trading day of the 3-Month Eurodollar futures contract. The minimum price movement for the futures option is .01 ($25). The exercise price intervals are .25 (0.25%). For example, you may see strikes of 95.50, 95.75, 96.00 etc. The option premium (price) is not paid at the time of purchase. According to *LIFFE's Summary of Futures and Options Contracts:*

> Option positions are marked-to-market daily. This marking-to-market generates positive or negative variation margin flows. If an option is exercised by the buyer, the buyer is required to pay the original contract price to the Clearing House and the Clearing House will pay the original option price to the seller on the following business day. Such payments are netted against the variation margin balances of the buyer and seller by the Clearing House.

This means that when a futures option on LIFFE is purchased, the buyer does not pay the option premium, but does post margin. LIFFE's margin schedule for July 27, 1995, indicates the amount of margin necessary for a 3-Month Eurodollar Futures Option is $500 (these requirements change periodically). This amount is called initial margin and is posted in the trader's margin account. The margin account will have a maintenance margin which is the level at which the trader must infuse more funds into his margin account due to losses. The additional amount that must be posted is called variation margin. Gains or losses accrue to the margin account as the futures option price changes. A decline in the put option's value is a loss to the option buyer but a gain to the seller. For example, suppose you purchased a put option with a premium of 0.74. If the put price drops to 0.72, this represents a loss to the option buyer of $1,000,000 x (.0002) x (90/360) = $50. Therefore his margin account will be reduced by this amount to $450. Conversely, the put seller's margin account will be increased by $50. This process is what is referred to as marking-to-market. If the option buyer's maintenance margin were $475, he would have to post variation margin of $25. Any amount in the margin account in excess of the initial margin may be withdrawn by the trader.

Descriptive Statistics for Real Data Set

Eurodollar futures options data provided by LIFFE cover the period from September of 1990 through July of 1994. Due to the size of this data set (143,636 observations) it was decided to examine the period covering January 1994 through July 1994. The first date for which trading information is available is January 4, 1994, and the last day is July 29, 1994. There are 10,231 observations for this period. Descriptive statistics for this data set are provided in Table 3.3. $R(t)$ is defined as the futures rate and is calculated as $100 - f(t)$ where $f(t)$ is the futures price. σ is the implied volatility as calculated by Black's (1976) futures option pricing model[5]. Implied volatility is that volatility which forces the option pricing model's calculated price to equal the observed market option price. v is used to denote the annualized volatility (standard deviation) of the futures rate and is calculated using:

$$PR_t = \frac{F_t}{F_{t-1}} \qquad (3.6a)$$

then

$$\overline{PR} = \frac{1}{T} \sum_{t=1}^{T} \ln\left(PR_t\right) \qquad (3.6b)$$

and

$$\sigma_{PR}^2 = \frac{1}{T-1} \sum \left(\ln\left(PR_t\right) - \overline{PR}\right)^2 \qquad (3.6c)$$

where PR_t is the price relative on day t, F_t is the futures rate on day t, F_{t-1} is the futures rate on day $t - 1$, and , is the variance of the price relative. For this study, the previous 60 trading days were used ($T = 60$) to compute the daily variance. Finally, the daily variance is used to compute the annualized volatility (standard deviation) as

$$v = \sqrt{250\sigma_{PR}^2},\qquad(3.6d)$$

where it is assumed that there are 250 trading days in a year. The remaining variables, τ, K, C, and P represent the option's maturity stated as a fraction of a year, the option's strike (exercise) price, market call price and market put price, respectively. Frequency distributions for the futures rate, annualized volatility, call option price, and put option price are provided in Figures 3.20–3.23.

From the Real Data Set a training data set and five different validation (holdout) sets were drawn. For the training set (TRAIN1), 2,000 values were randomly selected without replacement from the 8,887 observations in the Real Data set over the period January 4, 1994, through June 9, 1994 (observations for the rest of June were not available from LIFFE). The remaining observations over this time period were chosen as a validation sample (HOLDOUT1).

The HOLDOUT1 sample was drawn from the same data set as the training data set, TRAIN1, to test the trained GANNs ability to interpolate. To test the trained (optimized) GANNs ability to price options outside the training set (extrapolation), four additional validation samples were constructed. HOLDOUT2 consists of all observations over the period July 1 through July 8 and contains 384 observations. HOLDOUT3 consists of all observations over the period July 11 through July 15 and contains 320 observations. HOLDOUT4 and HOLDOUT5 cover the periods July 18 through July 22 and July 25 through July 29 respectively, and each contains 320 observations (all data sets are from 1994). Descriptive statistics for these samples are provided in Table 3.4.

Table 3.3: Descriptive Statistics for Real Data Set

Number of Observations: 10,231

	Mean	Standard Deviation	Skewness	Kurtosis	Minimum	Maximum
$R(t)$	5.113	0.916	-0.167	-1.154	3.340	6.710
v^{**}	32.272	13.941	2.147	3.525	14.349	72.555
σ^{*}	20.397	2.622	-0.159	0.158	8.650	26.60
τ	0.479	0.276	0.037	-1.212	0.008	0.981
Maturity**	174.796	100.622	0.037	-1.212	3	358
K	95.320	1.208	-0.177	-0.729	92.00	97.50
C	0.399	0.523	1.432	1.342	0.000	2.410
P	0.833	0.826	0.920	-0.131	0.000	3.300

* Volatility is stated as a percent. (20.39 = .2039)

** Maturity is stated in number of days.

$R(t)$ is the futures rate and is calculated as $100 - f(t)$ where $f(t)$ is the futures price. σ is the implied volatility as computed by Black's (1976) futures option pricing model while v is the annualized standard deviation of the underlying futures rate. τ is the option's maturity stated as a fraction of a year and K is the options strike (exercise) price. C and P are the reported call and put option prices respectively.

Figure 3.20

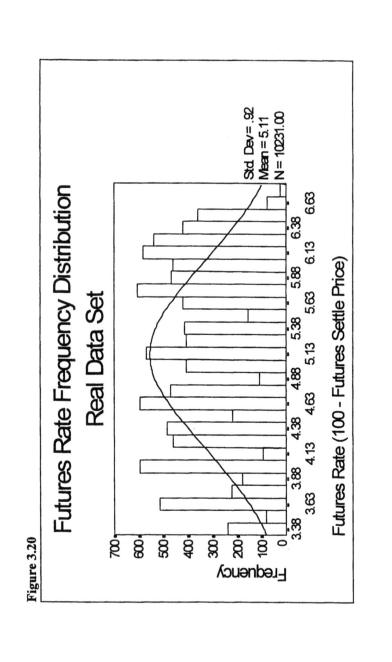

Futures Rate Frequency Distribution
Real Data Set

Figure 3.21

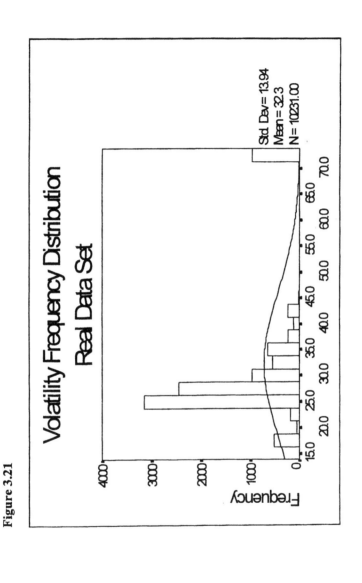

Volatility Frequency Distribution
Real Data Set

Std Dev = 13.94
Mean = 32.3
N = 10231.00

Figure 3.22

Call Option Price Frequency Distribution
Real Data Set

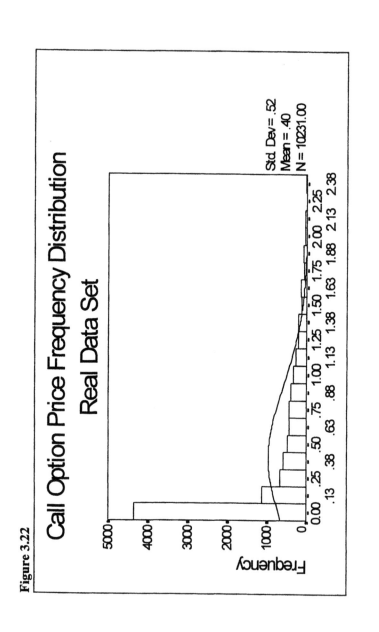

Figure 3.23

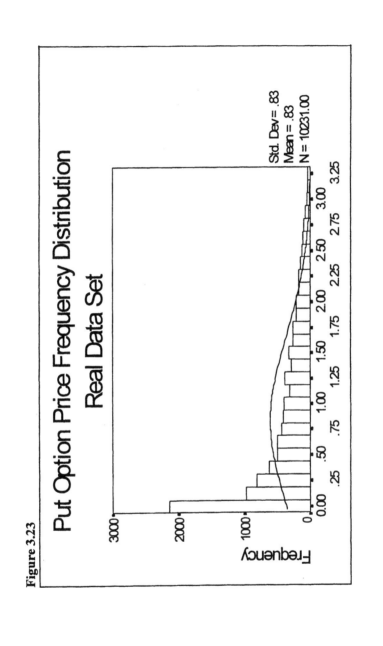

Put Option Price Frequency Distribution
Real Data Set

Std. Dev = .83
Mean = .83
N = 10231.00

SECTION III: NEURAL NETWORKS

Neural Networks have proven to be a valuable, if not controversial (at least among academics) tool in the field of finance. Neural network applications for finance currently being explored include: assessing the risk of mortgage loans [Collins, Ghosh, and Scofield (1988)]; rating the quality of corporate bonds [Dutta and Shekhar (1988)]; predicting financial distress [Salchenberger, Cinar and Lash (1992), Coats and Fant (1993) and Altman, et. al. (1994)]; predicting bond re-ratings [Hatfield and White (1998)]; and predicting fluctuations of stock price movements [Bower (1988)].

Financial forecasting seems to be an area particularly suited to neural networks. Yao, Li, and Tan (1997) utilized a simple backpropagation NN to forecast the Swiss Franc – U.S. dollar exchange rate and found the NN to be an adequate tool for forecasting. Yao, Li, and Tan used weekly data for their model and posited that more frequent data would have improved their results.

Pan, Liu, and Mejabi (1997) utilized a hybrid Neural Network-Fuzzy Logic system to forecast the S&P 500. The authors tested their model against traditional time series models including a random walk model, an ARIMA model, regression models and ARCH models. Their findings show the hybrid NN models to perform as well as or in many cases better than the traditional models.

According to Shandle (1993), companies such as General Electric, American Express, and Chase Manhattan Bank are using NNs to screen credit applications, spot stolen credit cards, and detect patterns which may indicate fraud. Shandle also reports that many brokerage house are using NNs to predict commodity and stock prices, bond ratings, and currency trading trends.

Neural networks have also been applied to options markets. Hutchinson, Lo, and Poggio (1994) apply a number of neural network models including radial basis function (RBF) networks and multilayer perceptron (MLP) networks to price S&P 500 futures options. The authors simulate Black-Scholes option prices and show that learning networks can approximate the B-S formula from a two-year training data set. They further use the trained networks to price and delta hedge[7] options. Hutchinson, Lo, and Poggio find that the learning networks were able to achieve error levels similar to those of the B-S formula.

Table 3.4: Descriptive Statistics for Real Data Set

Training and Holdout Samples

		$R(t)$	K	ν	τ	C	P
	Mean	4.96	4.57	31.905	0.470	0.40	0.79
TRAINONE	Std. Dev.	0.90	1.14	15.078	0.280	0.53	0.81
N=2000	Min	3.34	2.50	14.349	0.008	0.00	0.00
	Max	6.54	7.50	72.555	0.981	2.40	3.30
	Mean	4.98	4.56	31.653	0.450	0.40	0.82
HOLDOUT1	Std. Dev.	0.90	1.10	14.704	0.280	0.53	0.84
N=200	Min	3.34	2.50	14.349	0.011	0.00	0.00
	Max	6.54	7.25	72.555	0.973	2.06	3.15
	Mean	6.02	5.36	35.629	0.530	0.38	1.04
HOLDOUT2	Std. Dev.	0.47	1.37	4.640	0.270	0.45	0.86
N=384	Min	5.25	2.50	28.075	0.175	0.00	0.00
	Max	6.67	8.00	44.205	0.953	1.66	3.08
	Mean	5.99	5.36	36.317	0.510	0.38	1.01
HOLDOUT3	Std. Dev.	0.48	1.37	3.621	0.270	0.46	0.86
N=320	Min	5.11	2.50	31.629	0.156	0.00	0.00
	Max	6.71	8.00	41.626	0.926	1.79	3.12
	Mean	5.79	5.36	36.814	0.490	0.43	0.86

Table 3.4 (continued)

HOLDOUT3 N=320						
Std. Dev.	0.48	1.37	3.621	0.270	0.46	0.86
Min	5.11	2.50	31.629	0.156	0.00	0.00
Max	6.71	8.00	41.626	0.926	1.79	3.12
Mean	5.79	5.36	36.814	0.490	0.43	0.86

Training and Holdout Samples

	$R(t)$	K	v	τ	C	P
HOLDOUT4 N=320						
Std. Dev.	0.44	1.37	3.777	0.270	0.51	0.81
Min	5.07	2.50	30.247	0.137	0.00	0.00
Max	6.43	8.00	42.281	0.907	1.81	2.89
Mean	5.87	5.36	35.264	0.470	0.40	0.91
HOLDOUT5 N=320						
Std. Dev.	0.46	1.37	4.156	0.270	0.49	0.83
Min	5.05	2.50	30.001	0.118	0.00	0.00
Max	6.53	8.00	40.759	0.888	1.82	2.97

All variables are as previously defined.

Their out-of-sample tests show evidence that the learning networks outperform a naïve B-S model[8]. They conclude that the neural network approach is a promising alternative for pricing and hedging derivative securities when there is uncertainty about the specification of the underlying asset return process.

Lajbcygier et al (1997), utilize a hybrid neural network model with historical volatility to price and construct portfolios of real data on the Australian All Ordinaries Share Price Index. Both futures and futures options on the Australian Stock Exchange (ASX) All Ordinaries (AO) Share Price Index (SPI) trade on the Sydney Futures Exchange (SFE). The SFE futures options trade in a manner similar to the LIFFE options examined in this study in that both the buyer and seller post margin with the clearinghouse. Lajbcygier et al's hybrid neural network models are found to produce superior results when compared with traditional option pricing methodologies. A shortcoming of the hybrid models utilized was the persistence of systematic pricing errors. These pricing biases were similar to some of the biases found in the traditional OPM literature.

A neural network imitates neural biological functions in learning relationships between independent and dependent variables. A NN is therefore a simplified model of the human brain which is capable of learning and generalization. NNs are made up of processing elements (often called neurons, nodes, or cells) and connections which are organized in layers. Generally you have an input layer, one or more hidden layers and an output layer. A feedforward neural network has two or more layers, each of which gets input from the former layer. Output is then sent to the following layer. The NN takes a set of inputs and maps them to some set of outputs with the connections between neurons having some weight which influences an output cell. These weights are "learned" by the network through a process in which a training sample is presented to the network.

For this study a three layer (i.e. one middle or hidden layer) feedforward, neural network will be developed to approximate the process by which call and put option prices for options with futures-style margining are determined. This is a problem for which no closed form solutions exist (this is actually one of many types of options for which no closed form solutions exits). This NNs ability to forecast

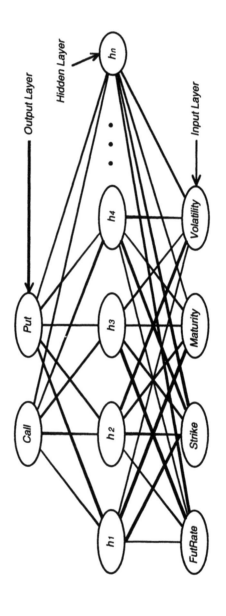

Figure 3.24 :A Multilayer Feedforward Neural Network

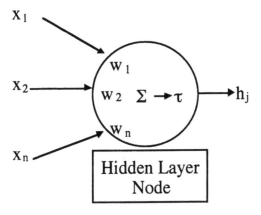

Figure 3.25

actual option prices will be tested and compared to existing option pricing methodologies. The inputs for the NN will be the same inputs which are used by existing methodologies. In particular, the inputs will be those that are used in the Chen & Scott model discussed above. Figure 3.24 shows a possible network structure utilizing the Chen & Scott inputs to produce call and put option prices.

Following White (1989), for a three layer network, any middle layer node will receive a weighted sum of all the input nodes plus a bias[6] and produces some output signal

$$h_j = \Phi\left(\sum_{i=1}^{n} w_{ij} x_i\right), \quad j = 1, \ldots, k, \ I = 0, \ldots, n, \qquad (3.6)$$

where ϕ is the transfer function, x_i is the ith input signal, w_{ij} is the strength of the connection from the ith input node to the jth middle layer node and h_j is the middle or hidden layer node.

The transfer function, ϕ, is applied to each neuron's activation value to generate each neuron's output. Many different types of functions can serve as the transferfunction. A typical transfer function is the non-linear, continuously differentiable sigmoid transfer function

$$\Phi(\theta) = \frac{1}{1 - e^{-\theta}},\tag{3.7}$$

which produces an S-shaped curve with values assigned between 0 and 1.

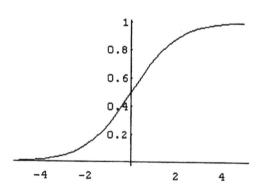

Figure 3. 26 Sigmoid Transfer Function

The signals for the hidden nodes are then sent to the output nodes in a similar fashion to Equation 3.6 above and produce a signal

$$o_k = \Phi\left(\sum_{j=1}^{q} b_j h_j\right), \tag{3.8}$$

where there are q hidden nodes, b_j is an output weight, o_k is the kth output node, and h_0 is always one so that b_0 provides a bias. By substituting equation (3.8) into (3.6) we have

$$y = \Phi\left(\sum_{j=0}^{q} b_j \Phi\left(\sum_{i=1}^{n} w_{ij} x_i\right)\right) = f(x, \theta), \tag{3.9}$$

where output (**y**) is shown as a function of the input vectors (**x**) and weights (**q**). White (1989) has shown that the output function

$$f(x, \theta) = \sum_{j=0}^{q} b_j \Phi\left(\sum_{i=1}^{n} w_{ij} x_i\right) \tag{3.10}$$

can provide an accurate approximation to any function of x provided q (the number of hidden nodes) is large enough. White further states that due to this property, "hidden-layer feedforward networks are useful for applications in pattern recognition, classification, forecasting, process control, and image compression and enhancement."

LEARNING METHOD

In order to learn, a NN needs to find weights (θ) that will approximate the underlying function. Many studies have utilized Back-propagation (BP) of Rumelhart et al. (1986) to accomplish this task [Salchenberger, Cinar and Lash (1992), Coates and Fant (1993), and Altman et al. (1994) to name a few]. Learning is accomplished through a Back-propagation Neural Network (BPNN) by taking the network's errors (BPNN output—actual values) and updating the connection weights using

$$\theta_t = \theta_{t-1} + \lambda \nabla f(X_t, \theta_{t-1})(Y_t - f(X_t, \theta_{t-1})), \quad t = 1, 2, \ldots, \quad (3.11)$$

where λ is a learning rate, ∇f is the gradient (vector of partial derivatives of f with respect to the weights, θ) and Y_t is the target outcome. The BPNN is therefore a point-to-point gradient-search technique. When a correct observation is encountered, weights are strengthened; and when errors are encountered, weights are weakened. Although BPNNs are widely used, they have a tendency to become stuck at local, rather than global, optimal solutions. Altman et al. (1994) found "illogical weightings of the indicators" in their corporate distress prediction comparison to Multiple Discriminant Analysis and Logit. In one case, they found that if the level of a firm's liquidity deteriorated (usually a bad sign), the NN showed an improvement in output. In some instances the improvement was enough to move what was an unsound firm into the category of healthy firms. This is clearly counter-intuitive. Although the NNs in Altman's study outperformed other prediction methods in many instances, he found the illogical weightings to be "unacceptable". It is possible that the illogical weightings could have been the result of the NN arriving at a local solution, as opposed to a global one. Another problem related to BPNNs is "overtraining". When overtraining occurs, the NN is not able to generalize (and therefore not able to predict well out-of-sample).

Because of the problems associated with BPNNs, the Genetic Algorithm (GA) optimization technique of Dorsey and Mayer (1994) will be utilized for network learning in this study. A GA uses evolutionary concepts in the optimization process. Because the GA is an intelligent global search technique, the problem of arriving at local optima is addressed. According to Kean (1995)

> GAs exceed other optimization procedures in robustness. Their advantage lies in a more thorough searching of a global solution space through avoidance of getting stuck at local optimums.

The GA was found to perform well when optimizing NNs by Dorsey, Johnson, and Mayer (1995). Furthermore, Sexton, Johnson, and Dorsey (1995) found the GA optimized NN to outperform the BPNN when testing out-of-sample, thereby addressing the problem of "overtraining".

A genetically optimized NN is trained by starting with a number of different sets of randomly selected weights (as opposed to one set with a BPNN). In keeping with the biological terminology, each of these sets may be thought of as a "chromosome" and the individual weights in a particular chromosome may be thought of as "genes". These "chromosomes" each represent a possible solution to the problem being analyzed. The NN is then trained with each set of weights (chromosomes) after which, the fitness of each chromosome in the initial population is evaluated (based on which sets of weights best minimized the objective function). Chromosomes with high levels of fitness are chosen as "parents" for the "reproduction" stage where a new generation of chromosomes is created to present to the network. The new generation is created through "crossover" and "mutation". Crossover is accomplished by combining the genes of two parent chromosomes (combining the weights of two parent weight vectors) in one or more pre-specified places. In this case, a point along two surviving weight vectors is randomly selected and the points to the left of that point are exchanged to produce two "child" vectors. One of the child vectors contains the weights of the first parent vector up to the crossover point and the weights of the second parent vector beyond the crossover point. The remaining child vector contains the complementary weights. The "offspring" chromosomes do not replace the parents, rather they replace the low fitting chromosomes. This process keeps the total population the same. The "reproduction" stage is illustrated in figure 3.27 below. Mutation is accomplished by assigning a random value to a randomly selected gene. The mutation process allows for increased robustness of the process. The new generation is then presented to the network, and the process continues until convergence.

With most predictive models the developer must specify the functional form of the relationship between the variables involved. For example, when applying Black's (1976) OPM to option pricing, the assumption that futures prices are lognormally distributed is required. With a neural network, knowledge of the true functional form of the underlying relationship is not necessary; and a neural network can be used to approximate any continuous function to any desired degree of accuracy, i.e. multilayer feedforward networks are universal approximators [Hornik, Stinchcombe, and White, (1989)]. Basically,

Figure 3.27

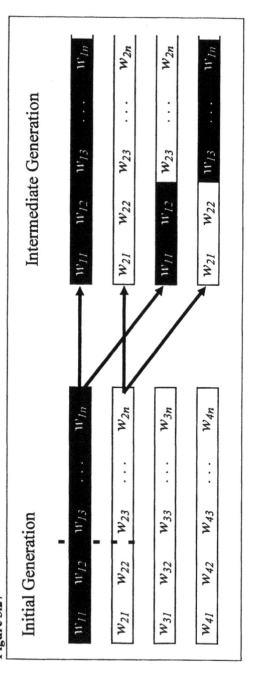

Figure 3.27 The "reproduction" stage used as part of the genetic algorithm. Reprinted by permission of the *Journal of Computational Intelligence in Finance*, March/April 1998, © 1998, Finance and Technology Publishing.

the NN is developing an internal representation of the relationship between the independent and dependent variables; and therefore, no a priori assumptions about the underlying distributions are necessary [Salchenberger, Cinar and Lash (1992)]. This characteristic can lead to reduced development time because the researcher doesn't have to spend time and resources trying to model the underlying relationships.

A further characteristic of NNs is generalization. Because a neural network can generalize, it can handle variations in inputs (such as partial or imperfect data) and still produce a correct output. Furthermore, according to Altman et al. (1994), NNs are able to handle imprecise variables and changes in model relationships over time. Therefore, the NN is able to adapt gradually to the appearance of new cases which may contain valuable information about possible changes in the relationships among variables.

Neural networks do have their disadvantages. One of the criticisms of neural networks is that the internal structure of the model is unknown. According to Eliot (1995):

> One of the traditional disadvantages of neural networks is the incredible complexity of the neural interconnections' internal nuances and their logical meaning in terms of the problem to be solved. In most instances, users can only inspect and understand the output of the neural network, while the internal guts are treated as a mysterious black box that magically (and hopefully) generates the right kinds of outputs for the inputs provided.

Thus, most reliability tests of NNs have been limited to examining the NN's output. Other objections to neural networks include the large computational resources necessary and the lack of a formal theory for determining the optimal network topology [Salchenberger, Cinar and Lash (1991)].

NOTES

1. The choice of this process is rather ad hoc. A process for the futures price, $F(t)$, could have been chosen as was done by Black (1976). The goal here was to simply generate observations, however, and not develop a model for futures rates.

2. Again, as with futures rates, the choice of this process is ad hoc and used simply to generate data.

3. It should be noted that Chen and Scott (1993) incorrectly specified their model by failing to reverse the signs for the d_1 and d_2 variables in their call option pricing model.

4. Eurodollar futures are quoted as a percent of face value of the underlying. Therefore, a futures price if 97.23 represents 97.23% of $1 million. A 0.01 tick move then equates to $1,000,000 (90/360)(0.0001) = $25.

5. The implied volatilities were supplied by LIFFE.

6. According to White (1989), this bias can be interpreted as coming from an input x_0 that always has the value one.

7. The delta of a derivative security refers to the sensitivity of a derivative security's price in relation to the price of the underlying security. A neutral delta hedged portfolio is one that is constructed in such a manner that a small change in the underlying security's value will not affect the portfolio's value. This is because gains (losses) in the derivative securities exactly offset losses (gains) in the underlying asset.

8. Hutchinson, Lo, and Poggio limit their study to call options only.

CHAPTER IV

Results

In this chapter, the empirical results of the neural network approximations of simulated and real call and put option prices are presented. In the first section, the results of the simulation will be discussed. In addition the Genetic Adaptive Neural Networks (GANNs) ability to approximate a known option pricing function is tested. Further, the GANNs results will be tested to determine if the weightings are "logical" (i.e. does an increase in the degree of moneyness[1] lead to the logical conclusion of an increase in the option's value). The results for calls will be presented first, followed by the results for puts.

The GANNs ability to accurately price the options on 3-month Eurodollar futures listed on LIFFE will be presented in the second section. The GANNs results will be compared to the actual market prices and to the predicted prices of Chen & Scott's (1993) modification of the Black-Scholes formula (denoted BS_{CS} OPM). First the GANN will be tested using the same variables as inputs that the BS_{CS} OPM uses (namely, the Futures Rate ($F(t)$), the Strike Rate ($100 - K$), the annualized volatility of the underlying futures contract (u) and time to maturity (t)). Secondly, the GANN will be tested using additional information (namely, the 3-month Eurodollar rate ($EU03$) and a measure of the degree of moneyness (M)) as inputs. This is done because all option pricing models tend to produce pricing biases indicating model misspecification or the omission of relevant economic variables. One of the strengths of the GANN is its ability to easily incorporate additional inputs.

SECTION I: SIMULATION RESULTS

As was outlined in the previous chapter, 40,500 call and put option prices were generated using the Chen & Scott (1993) modification of the basic Black-Scholes option pricing formula. This was done so that the GANN could be tested in a controlled environment, where the process that determines the option values was known, and all the relevant input variables were also known. Out of this population of 40,500 simulation observations, 4,000 observations were selected randomly as a training data set for the GANN. The remaining 36,500 observations were chosen as a validation, or holdout, data set. Some of these observations were dropped because the simulation generation process led to a small number of option values that were negative due to rounding beyond 14 decimal places. It was decided to drop these observations rather than "force" them to be zero. This left 3,991 observations in the training data set and 36,412 observations in the validation data set.

A number of different network topologies were developed and trained. The training process usually consisted of training the GANN for 100 generations, followed by a 1000 generation training run to ensure that the network was training properly. Once it was determined that the network was training adequately, the GANNs were trained 100,000 generations, in steps of 10,000. Each time a new 10,000 generation run was started, it used the "best" weights from the previous run as a starting point. The GANNs objective function was to minimize sum of squared errors (SSE), so the set of weights that provided the smallest SSE was chosen as the "best" weights.

All of the networks developed had one input layer, one hidden or middle layer, and one output layer. The input layer consisted of the four inputs that were used to generate the simulation prices for all the networks tested. These inputs were the futures rate ($F(t)$), the strike rate ($100 - K$), the time to maturity (t) and volatility (s). All of the GANN's had a single node in the output layer. This was either the simulated call price or the simulated put price. Therefore, for each neural network structure tested, there were two GANNs developed; one to price call options and one to price put options.

The differences in the GANNs tested were related to the objective function and the number of hidden layer nodes. A number of different neural network structures were tested, where the number of hidden layer nodes was increased from 10 to 20. The models with fewer than 15 hidden nodes provided only marginal performance in terms of minimization of SSE. The models that had more than 15 hidden nodes tended to take very long to train and the additional reduction in SSE tended to be small. As mentioned in the previous chapter, a neural network can theoretically approximate any underlying function to any degree of accuracy desired, provided the number of hidden layer nodes is large enough. Adding hidden layer nodes is not cost-less, however, as doing so increases the time necessary to train a network and increases the likelihood that the neural network may "overfit" to the training data set, resulting in poor performance out-of-sample.

A number of networks were developed whose objective function was to minimize the sum of absolute errors (SAE). This was done because of the possibility that an objective function of minimizing SSE could lead the neural network to give higher priority to correcting outliers which produce large squared error terms. If this is the case, then a network whose objective function was to minimize SAE could possibly provide superior performance. However, these models tended to underperform the networks whose objective function was to minimize SSE, both in terms of SSE and SAE.

After examining the different network structures developed, it was determined that the GANNs which provided superior performance for this particular data set were those with 15 hidden layer nodes and whose objective function was to minimize SSE. Consequently, there were two networks chosen for further experimentation (one for pricing calls and one for pricing puts). These networks were then trained an additional 30,000 generations in a "fine-tuning" process.

CALL OPTIONS

Training Sample

The results of GANNs ability to accurately price call options in the simulation training data set are presented in Table 4.1. In this table, the Mean Squared Error (MSE) and Mean Absolute Error (MAE) are reported. Error terms were calculated as the target price (the simulation call price, C_S) minus the neural network predicted call price (C_{GANN}). The data set is divided into a number of sub-samples based on whether or not the option is in-the-money, at-the-money, or out-of-the-money. The term M is used as a measure of the degree of moneyness and is calculated as the strike rate minus the futures rate $((100 - K) - F(t))$ for call options. If the strike rate is greater than the futures rate, then a call option will be in-the-money. If the strike rate is less than the futures rate, then a call option will be out of the money (recall from the previous chapter that a call on a futures rate is equivalent to a put on the futures price). Therefore, a call option was in-the-money if $M > .01$, out-of-the-money if $M < -.01$, and at-the-money is $-.01 < M < .01$.

The sample was further divided based on "how far" the option was in-the-money or out-of-the-money. If $M > .01$ but $M < 1.5$, the option was labeled just in-the-money. If $M > 1.5$, the option was labeled deep in-the-money. If $M < -.01$ but $M > -1.5$, the option was labeled just out-of-the-money. If $M < -1.5$, the option was labeled deep out-of-the-money.

The results for the entire sample (3991 observations) indicate a MSE and MAE of 0.00016 and 0.00944 respectively. Using the MAE, this implies that, on average, the GANN will misprice a call option by 0.00944. For all in-the-money calls (including deep in-the-money, 2014 observations) the MSE and MAE are 0.00014 and 0.00878, while for all out-of-the-money calls (including deep out-of-the-money, 1950 observations) the MSE and MAE are 0.00018 and 0.00994. Thus, the GANN appears to do a better job of pricing in-the-money calls over out-of-the-money and at-the-money calls (MSE = 0.00067 and MAE = 0.02078).

In examining the in-the-money category, the GANN tended to price deep in-the-money options ($M > 1.5$) better than just in-the-money options ($0.01 < M < 1.5$). The neural network also priced just out-of-the-money options ($-1.5 < M < -.01$) better than deep out-of-the-money options ($M < -1.5$). As a whole, the GANN performed well when approximating the simulated call option prices and had the smallest MAE when pricing deep in-the-money calls. The largest MAE occurred when approximating at-the-money calls.

Additional tests were conducted to determine if the observed errors were significant (i.e. to see if the GANN predicted price was significantly different from the BS_{CS} OPM price). To implement this, both parametric and non-parametric tests were employed. The results of this analysis are presented in Table 4.2. First a simple paired-sample *t*-test is employed to test the following hypothesis:

Table 4.1: Results Of Genetic Adaptive Neural Network (GANN) Approximation Of The Chen & Scott Modified Black-Scholes Formula (BS$_{CS}$ OPM) (Simulation Training Data Set: Calls)

Sub-sample Description	Number of Observations	Mean Squared Error (MSE)	Mean Absolute Error (MAE)
Complete Sample	3991	0.00016	0.00944
$M^* > .01$	2014	0.00014	0.00878
$.01 < M < 1.5$	1312	0.00175	0.01015
$M > 1.5$	702	0.00008	0.00627
$M < -.01$	1950	0.00018	0.00994
$-1.5 < M < -.01$	1249	0.00017	0.00993
$M < -1.5$	701	0.00020	0.00996
$-.01 < M < .01$	27	0.00067	0.02078

Source: Reprinted by permission of the *Journal of Computational Intelligence in Finance*, February/March 1998, © 1998, Finance and Technology Publishing.

$^*M$ is a measure of the degree of moneyness. For example, if the strike rate $(100 - K)$ is greater than the futures rate $(F(t))$, a call option on a 3-month Eurodollar futures contract will be in-the-money. Therefore, M is defined as $(100 - K) - F(t)$, and when $M > .01$ the call option is in-the-money.

Table 4.2: Comparison Of Simulation And Genetic Adaptive Neural Network Prices For Call Options (Paired Sample t-test, Training Sample)

Sub-sample Description	Number of Observations	Average Simulation Price (C_S)	Average GANN Price (C_{GANN})	Mean D^*	t-value	2-tailed Significance
Complete Sample	3991	0.6748	0.6748	0.0000	0.00	1.000
M** > .01	2014	1.2941	1.2937	-0.0004	-1.39	0.165
.01 < M < 1.5	1312	0.8356	0.8357	0.0001	0.36	0.720
M > 1.5	702	2.1511	2.1498	-0.0013	-3.92	0.000
M < -.01	1950	0.0411	0.0414	0.0003	0.94	0.345
-1.5 < M < -.01	1249	0.0638	0.0648	0.0009	2.52	0.012
M < -1.5	701	0.0007	-0.0002	-0.0009	-1.61	0.107
-.01 < M < .01	27	0.2374	0.2441	0.0067	1.36	0.186

Table 4.2 (continued)

Sub-sample Description	Number of Observations	Mean - Rank	Mean + Rank	Cases-Ranks/+ Ranks	Z-value	2-tailed Significance
Complete Sample	3991	2,011.92	1,980.64	1960/2031	-0.5448	0.5859
M** > .01	2014	1,025.46	991.87	937/1077	-2.0572	0.0397
.01 < M < 1.5	1312	642.89	671.74	693/916	-1.0823	0.2791
M > 1.5	702	348.52	353.09	244/458	-7.1325	0.0000
M < -.01	1950	970.64	980.70	1008/942	-1.0977	0.2723
-1.5 < M < -.01	1249	639.81	607.87	670/579	-3.0084	0.0026
M < -1.5	701	332.09	368.61	338/363	-2.0096	0.0445
-.01 < M < .01	27	15.40	12.25	15/12	-1.0091	0.3130

Source: Reprinted by permission of the *Journal of Computational Intelligence in Finance*, February/March 1998, © 1998, Finance and Technology Publishing.

* D = Average difference in predicted value from actual value ($C_{GANN} - C_S$). ** M = degree of moneyness (($100 - K$) - $F(t)$). The term -*Ranks* refers to cases where $C_S > C_{GANN}$, while +*Ranks* refers to cases where $C_S < C_{GANN}$.

H$_0$:   The GANN call option price is the same as the simulation call option price. Alternatively, $D = 0$.

H$_1$:   The GANN call option price is not the same as the simulation call option price. Alternatively, $D = 0$.

D is the difference in the neural network's predicted price and the simulation price ($C_{GANN} - C_S$). The t value is then calculated as:

$$t = \frac{\overline{D}}{S_{\overline{D}}},$$ (4.1a)

where,

$$\overline{D} = \frac{1}{n} \sum_{i=1}^{n} D_i,$$ (4.1b)

$$S_{\overline{D}} = \frac{S_D}{\sqrt{n}},$$ (4.1c)

and

$$S_D = \sqrt{\frac{\sum D^2 - \frac{\left(\sum D^2\right)}{n}}{n-1}}.$$ (4.1d)

In the above equations, n is the number of pairs, or observations of D.

Secondly, a non-parametric test was employed. The Wilcoxon signed-ranks test may be used to replace the paired-difference t-test when the assumption of normality is not satisfied. Examination of normal probability plots and detrended normal plots for the D variable indicate that it is not normally distributed. Furthermore, the Lilliefors test for normality leads to the rejection of the hypothesis that the D variable is normally distributed[2]. The results for the t-test indicate that in only one instance (deep in-the-money) can the hypothesis that $D = 0$ be rejected at the .01 level. At a .05 level of significance, the hypothesis of no difference in the GANN price and the target price can be rejected for the case of just out-of-the-money calls. The evidence for the entire sample (3991 observations) and the remaining sub-samples precludes the rejection of the hypothesis that there is no difference in the GANN approximation and the simulated call price.

Using the Wilcoxon test, the hypothesis that $D = 0$ can be rejected at the .01 level only for the sub-samples of deep in-the-money calls and just out-of-the money calls. At a .05 level of significance we could also reject the hypothesis that $D = 0$ for the deep out-of-the-money calls and for all in-the-money calls. For the remaining sub-samples, the hypothesis of equivalence between the GANN approximation and the simulated price cannot be rejected.

Overall, these results indicate that we cannot conclude that the call prices predicted by the GANN are significantly different from the simulation prices except in the cases of deep in-the-money calls and just out-of-the-money calls. These results suggest that the Genetic Adaptive Neural Network has indeed done a good job of approximating a complex, non-linear, call option valuation function.

Empirical studies of traditional option pricing models have found these models to exhibit pricing biases. For example, the Black-Scholes model has been found to systematically misprice options that are deep out-of-the-money puts or deep in-the-money, or that have a long time to maturity. A way to test for the existence of pricing bias is to regress the difference in the observed price from the actual price against whatever variable you believe may produce a bias. To test for pricing bias, regressions were conducted on the degree of moneyness (M), time to expiration (t), and the volatility of the underlying futures rate (s). The results of the regressions are presented in Table 4.3. The dependent variable of each regression equation is the difference between the simulated call price and the GANN estimated price (D).

Referring to Table 4.3, none of the explanatory variables are significant in any of the three regression equations. Therefore, the results imply that the moneyness bias, the maturity bias, and the volatility bias do not exist in the training data set for call options.

VALIDATION SAMPLE

Once training was completed, the trained GANNs were presented with new data in order to test the ability of the Neural Networks to price options out-of-sample. The results of the GANNs ability to accurately price call options in the validation data set are presented in Table 4.4. In this table, all variables are as previously described, and the data set is divided into sub-samples based on the degree of moneyness.

The results for the entire sample (36,412 observations) indicate a MSE and MAE of 0.00017 and 0.00953, respectively. There were 18,408 in-the-money calls and this category had a MSE of 0.00015 and a MAE of 0.00914. For all out-of-the-money calls (17,806 observations) the MSE and MAE are 0.00018 and 0.00988, while for all at-the-money calls (198 observations) the MSE and MAE are 0.00037 and 0.01431.

For the in-the-money category, the results are similar to the training sample results. The GANN priced deep in-the-money options (M > 1.5) better than just in-the-money options (0.01 < M < 1.5). The MAE for the deep in-the-money category is 0.00672, indicating that, on average, the GANN will missprice a deep in-the-money call option by 0.00672.

For pricing out-of-the-money call options, there was little difference between the GANN's ability to price deep out-of-the-money or just out-of-the-money calls. In terms of MAE, the GANN performed slightly better with deep out-of-the-moneys while in terms of MSE the GANN performed slightly better on just out-of-the-money calls.

On the whole, the GANN performed well when pricing call options out of sample and had the smallest MAE when pricing deep in-the-money calls. These results are similar to the training sample results. Also, as with the training sample, the largest MAE occurred when approximating at-the-money calls.

As with the training sample, additional tests were conducted to determine if the observed errors were significant. Because examination of normal probability plots and detrended normal plots for the D variable indicated non-normality, both parametric and non-parametric tests were employed. The results of the tests for significance are presented in Table 4.5.

Upon examining Table 4.5, it is clear that the hypothesis that the neural network approximation is the same as the simulated call price cannot be rejected for the entire sample (36,412 observations). This is the case for both the paired sample t-test and the Wilcoxon matched-pairs signed-ranks test, as evidenced by the large p-values. The

Table 4.3: OLS Regression Results Of Pricing Errors On Selected Parameters (Simulation Training Data Set: Calls, N = 3991)

Equation	α	βM	$\beta \tau$	$\beta \sigma$	R^2
$D = \alpha + \beta M + \varepsilon$	-2.576E-09 (-0.000)	5.296E-08 (0.000)			0.00000
$D = \alpha + \beta \tau + \varepsilon$	3.294E-07 (0.001)		-8.025E-07 (-0.001)		0.00000
$D = \alpha + \beta \sigma + \varepsilon$	7.139E-06 (0.001)			-3.423E-05 (-0.001)	0.00000

Note: $D = C_{GANN} - C_S$ (or neural network call price - target call price), M = degree of moneyness $((100 - K) - F(t))$, t = time to maturity, and s = volatility measure.

The terms a and b are the regression coefficients and e is the error term.

All t-statistics are below their respective coefficients in parentheses.

Table 4.4: Results Of Genetic Adaptive Neural Network (GANN) Approximation Of The Chen & Scott Modified Black-Scholes Formula (BS$_{CS}$) (Simulation Validation Data Set: Calls)

Sub-sample Description	Number of Observations	Mean Squared Error (MSE)	Mean Absolute Error (MAE)
Complete Sample	36412	0.00017	0.00953
$M^* > .01$	18408	0.00015	0.00914
$.01 < M < 1.5$	11972	0.00019	0.01044
$M > 1.5$	6436	0.00008	0.00672
$M < -.01$	17806	0.00018	0.00988
$-1.5 < M < -.01$	11432	0.00017	0.00991
$M < -1.5$	6374	0.00019	0.00984
$-.01 < M < .01$	198	0.00037	0.01431

Source: Reprinted by permission of the *Journal of Computational Intelligence in Finance*, February/March 1998, © 1998, Finance and Technology Publishing.

* M is a measure of the degree of moneyness. For example, if the strike rate $(100 - K)$ is greater than the futures rate $(F(t))$, a call option on a 3-month Eurodollar futures contract will be in-the-money. Therefore, M is defined as $(100 - K) - F(t)$, and when $M > .01$ the call option is in-the-money.

differences do appear significant for some of the sub-samples however. The hypothesis that $D = 0$ can be rejected at the .01 level for the deep in-the-money $(M > 1.5)$, out-of-the-money $(M < -.01)$, and just out-of-the-money sub-samples $(-1.5 < M < -.01)$, whether using parametric or non-parametric tests. In addition, for the in-the-money category $(M > .01)$, the D variable appears to be significantly different from zero at the .05 level for the parametric test and at the .01 level for the non-parametric test. Although the at-the-money category $(-.01 < M < .01)$ had the largest error (as measured by MAE), the difference was not statistically significant at the .01 level.

These results indicate that the call prices approximated by the GANN are not significantly different from the simulation call prices for all of the sub-samples. Although the pricing errors do appear to be statistically significant for some of the sub-samples, as a whole there is

Table 4.5: Comparison Of Simulation And Genetic Adaptive Neural Network Prices For Call Options (Paired Sample t-test, Validation Sample)

Sub-sample Description	Number of Observations	Average Simulation Price (C_S)	Average GANN Price (C_{GANN})	Mean D*	t-value	2-tailed Significance
Complete Sample	36412	0.6776	0.6777	0.0001	1.16	0.246
M** > .01	18408	1.2944	1.2942	-0.0002	-2.46	0.014
.01 < M < 1.5	11972	0.8312	0.8312	0.0000	-0.18	0.858
M > 1.5	6436	2.1560	2.1554	-0.0006	-5.23	0.000
M < -.01	17806	0.0446	0.0450	0.0004	4.05	0.000
-1.5 < M < -.01	11432	0.0691	0.0696	0.0005	4.16	0.000
M < -1.5	6374	0.0007	0.0009	0.0002	1.30	0.193
-.01 < M < .01	198	0.2576	0.2566	-0.0009	-0.68	0.498

Table 4.5 (continued)

Sub-sample Description	Number of Observations	Mean - Rank	Mean + Rank	Cases -Ranks/+ Ranks	Z-value	2-tailed Significance
Complete Sample	36412	18344.20	18055.34	18039/18357	-0.1324	0.8947
$M** > .01$	18,408	9357.54	9061.06	8716/9686	-4.3054	0.0000
$.01 < M < 1.5$	11972	5868.53	6111.07	6222/5747	-1.8435	0.0652
$M > 1.5$	6436	3300.72	3163.99	2494/3939	-14.2014	0.0000
$M < -.01$	17806	8884.30	8913.82	9244/8552	-4.3012	0.0000
$-1.5 < M < -.01$	11432	5768.87	5654.98	5972/5456	-5.1010	0.0000
$M < -1.5$	6374	3132.16	3239.81	3272/3096	-0.7428	0.4576
$-.01 < M < .01$	198	100.98	98.52	79/119	-2.3200	0.0203

Source: Reprinted by permission of the *Journal of Computational Intelligence in Finance*, February/March 1998, © 1998, Finance and Technology Publishing.

* D = Average difference in predicted value from actual value (C_{GANN} - C_S), ** M = degree of moneyness ($(100 - K) - F(t)$). The term -*Ranks* refers to cases where $C_S > C_{GANN}$, while +*Ranks* refers to cases where $C_S < C_{GANN}$.

insufficient evidence to conclusively state that the GANN approximations are significantly different from the observed simulation call prices.

As with the training sample, regressions were conducted on the degree of moneyness (M), the time to expiration (t), and the volatility of the underlying futures rate (s) in order to test for the existence of pricing bias. The ordinary-least-squares (OLS) regression results are presented in Table 4.6.

Referring to Table 4.6, all explanatory variables are significant at the .01 level. This implies that the moneyness bias, maturity bias, and volatility bias exist with the GANN call option price approximations. Although the R^2 values are small, this does not mean that there is no association among the variables. A low R^2 simply indicates that there is no linear relationship present. These results are similar to the findings of other futures options studies, in particular, Whaley (1986) and Shastri and Tandon (1986). Shastri and Tandon (1986) found evidence of a moneyness and maturity bias when utilizing Geske and Johnson's (1984) OPM to approximate S&P and German Mark futures options. Whaley (1986) found evidence of a moneyness and maturity bias in pricing S&P equity futures options using analytic approximation models.

In summarizing the results for the call option pricing simulation, the evidence precludes the uniform rejection of the hypothesis tested. Thus, the GANN has been able to accurately approximate the simulated call option prices. Although statistically significant differences can be found in some sub-samples, the differences are not significant for the sample as a whole, nor are they significant for all of the sub-samples. The results are similar for both the training sample and the validation sample, which implies that the GANN was not merely memorizing the training sample ("overfitting" to the training data). Although there appear to be pricing biases in the validation sample, the magnitude of the errors is small as measured by MAE and MSE. The MAE was less than .01 for all sub-samples with the exception of the at-the-money (-.01 < M < .01) and just in-the-money (.01 < M < 1.5) sub-samples. On the whole, the evidence indicates that the GANN performed quite well when approximating a complex, non-linear call option valuation function.

Table 4.6: OLS Regression Results Of Pricing Errors On Selected Parameters (Simulation Validation Data Set: Calls, N = 36412)

Equation	α	βM	$\beta \tau$	$\beta \sigma$	R^2
$D = \alpha + \beta M + \varepsilon$	8.304E-05	-1.323E-04			0.00022
	(1.233)	(-2.853)			
$D = \alpha + \beta \tau + \varepsilon$	-4.227E-04		0.001216		0.00040
	(-2.874)		(3.830)		
$D = \alpha + \beta \sigma + \varepsilon$	-0.005260			0.025585	0.00019
	(-2.568)			(2.608)	

Note: $D = C_{GANN} - C_S$ (or neural network call price - target call price), M = degree of moneyness ($(100 - K) - F(t)$), τ = time to maturity, and σ = volatility measure.

The terms α and β are the regression coefficients and e is the error term.

All t-statistics are below their respective coefficients in parentheses.

PUT OPTIONS

Training Sample

The results of the GANN's ability to approximate put option prices in the simulation training data set are presented in Table 4.7. Error terms were calculated as the neural network predicted put price (P_{GANN}) minus the target price (the simulation put price, P_S). The measures MSE and MAE are as previously described. The moneyness measure (M) is computed as the futures rate minus the strike rate ($F(t) - (100 - K)$). This is different from the calculation for call options because if the strike rate is greater than the futures rate, then a put option will be out-of-the-money. If the strike rate is less than the futures rate, then a put option will be in-the-money (a put on a futures rate is equivalent to a call on the futures price). By calculating the degree of moneyness measure (M) in this manner, the interpretation of the calculation is the same as it was for call options. That is, for a put option, $M > .01$ implies in-the-money, $M < .01$ implies out-of-the-money and so on. The sample was also divided based on "how far" the option was in-the-money or out-of-the-money as was done with the call option sample.

Table 4.7: Results Of Genetic Adaptive Neural Network (GANN) Approximation Of The Chen & Scott Modified Black-Scholes Formula (BS$_{CS}$ OPM) (Simulation Training Data Set: Puts)

Sub-sample Description	Number of Observations	Mean Squared Error (MSE)	Mean Absolute Error (MAE)
Complete Sample	3991	0.00022	0.01083
$M^* > .01$	1950	0.00020	0.01025
$.01 < M < 1.5$	1249	0.00023	0.01147
$M > 1.5$	701	0.00014	0.00809
$M < -.01$	2014	0.00022	0.01122
$-1.5 < M < -.01$	1312	0.00023	0.01126
$M < -1.5$	702	0.00021	0.01114
$-.01 < M < .01$	27	0.00074	0.02444

* M is a measure of the degree of moneyness. For example, if the futures rate ($F(t)$) is greater than the strike rate ($100 - K$), a put option on a 3-month Eurodollar futures contract will be in-the-money. Therefore, M is defined as $F(t) - (100 - K)$, and when $M > .01$ the put option is in-the-money.

Referring to Table 4.7, the errors are marginally larger for all categories than they were for call options. For the entire sample (3991 observations) the MSE and MAE are 0.00022 and 0.01083, as compared to 0.00016 and 0.00944 for calls. Using MAE this implies that, on average, the GANN will missprice a put option by 0.01083. For all in-the-money puts (1950 observations), the MSE and MAE are 0.00020 and 0.01025, while for all out-of-the-money puts (2014 observations) the MSE and MAE are 0.00022 and 0.01122. For at-the-money puts, those numbers are 0.00074 and 0.02444, respectively. Thus, as with call options, the GANN appears to do a better job of approximating in-the-money puts over out-of-the-money and at-the-money puts.

In reviewing the in-the-money category, the GANN tended to approximate deep in-the-money puts ($M > 1.5$) better than just in-the-money puts ($.01 < M < 1.5$). As for out-of-the-money puts, the neural network approximated deep out-of-the-money options ($M < -1.5$) better than just out-of-the-money options ($-1.5 < M < -.01$). As a whole, the GANN performed well when approximating the simulated put option prices. As with the call options, the GANN had the smallest MAE when pricing deep in-the-money options and the largest MAE when pricing at-the-money options.

As was done with call options, supplementary tests were performed to determine if the observed pricing errors were statistically significant. The hypothesis tested was:

H_0:   The GANN put option price is the same as the simulation put option price. Alternatively, $D = 0$.

H_1:   The GANN put option price is not the same as the simulation put price. Alternatively, $D = 0$.

The variable D is the difference in the neural network's predicted price and the simulation price ($P_{GANN} - P_S$). All other calculations are as previously described. Because examination of normal probability plots and detrended normal plots for the D variable indicated that it was not normally distributed, both parametric and non-parametric tests were employed. The results of the tests for significance are presented in Table 4.8.

Table 4.8: Comparison Of Simulation And Genetic Adaptive Neural Network Prices For Put Options (Panel A: Paired Sample t-test, Training Sample)

Sub-sample Description	Number of Observations	Average Simulation Price (Ps)	Average GANN Price (PGANN)	Mean D*	t-value	2-tailed Significance
Complete Sample	3991	0.6419	0.6419	0.0000	0.00	0.997
M** > .01	1950	1.2561	1.2562	0.0001	0.23	0.817
.01 < M < 1.5	1249	0.7944	0.7948	0.0004	0.92	0.358
M > 1.5	701	2.0788	2.0783	-0.0005	-1.10	0.273
M < -.01	2014	0.0525	0.0524	-0.0001	-0.44	0.661
-1.5 < M < -.01	1312	0.0789	0.0794	0.0005	1.09	0.274
M < -1.5	702	0.0032	0.0019	-0.0013	-2.33	0.020
-.01 < M < .01	27	0.2386	0.2443	0.0057	1.02	0.318

Table 4.8 (continued)

Sub-sample Description	Number of Observations	Mean - Rank	Mean + Rank	Cases -Ranks/+ Ranks	Z-value	2-tailed Significance
Complete Sample	3991	1953.92	2039.85	2082/1907	-1.2239	0.2210
$M^{**} > .01$	1950	989.22	961.64	944/1005	-0.6564	0.5116
$.01 < M < 1.5$	1249	649.98	602.71	589/660	-0.5863	0.5577
$M > 1.5$	701	347.50	353.58	355/345	-0.1287	0.8976
$M < -.01$	2014	945.25	1084.92	1123/890	-1.8392	0.0659
$-1.5 < M < -.01$	1312	615.28	720.49	798/514	-4.3953	0.0000
$M < -1.5$	702	332.51	366.98	325/376	-2.7893	0.0053
$-.01 < M < .01$	27	15.07	12.67	15/12	-0.8889	0.3740

Source: Reprinted by permission of the *Journal of Computational Intelligence in Finance*, February/March 1998, © 1998, Finance and Technology Publishing.

* D = Average difference in predicted value from actual value ($P_{GANN} - P_S$), ** M = degree of moneyness ($F(t) - (100 - K)$). The term -*Ranks* refers to cases where $P_S > P_{GANN}$, while +*Ranks* refers to cases where $P_S < P_{GANN}$.

Although the errors were marginally larger for the put simulation training data set than for the call simulation training data set, there were fewer instances of significance in the former when utilizing the paired sample t-test. The hypothesis of equivalence between the GANN put approximation and the simulated put price cannot be rejected at the .01 level for the entire sample (3991 observations) or for any of the sub-samples. At the .05 level, the hypothesis of equivalence can be rejected for the deep out-of-the-money category ($M < -1.5$) only. For the remaining categories, the large p-values (2-tailed significance column) imply a lack of significance.

Using the Wilcoxon test, the hypothesis that $D = 0$ can be rejected at the .01 level for the case of just out-of-the-money ($-1.5 < M < -.01$) and deep out-of-the-money puts ($M < -1.5$) only. For the complete sample (3991 observations), the in-the-money ($M > .01$), at-the-money ($-.01 < M < .01$) and out-of-the-money ($M < -.01$) categories, the hypothesis of equivalence cannot be rejected. Furthermore, the hypothesis of equivalence cannot be rejected for any of the in-the-money sub-samples.

Altogether, the evidence suggests that the hypothesis $D = 0$ cannot be rejected except in the case of deep out-of-the-money puts and, possibly, just out-of-the-money puts. Therefore, the conclusion is that the GANN put prices are not significantly different from the simulated put prices. These results show that the GANN has been able to approximate, to a high degree of accuracy, the put option pricing function used to generate the simulated prices.

Regressions were utilized to test for the existence of pricing biases. As with call options, regressions were conducted on the degree of moneyness, time to expiration, and the volatility of the underlying futures rate. The dependent variable of each regression equation is the difference between the simulated put price and the GANN estimated price. The results of the regressions are presented in Table 4.9. Although there is no evidence to support the existence of a moneyness bias or a volatility bias, there does appear to be a time to maturity bias as evidenced by a t-statistic that is significant at the .01 level. The negative coefficient for the t variable implies a tendency for the GANN to underprice put options with longer terms to maturity in the training sample.

Table 4.9: OLS Regression Results Of Pricing Errors On Selected Parameters (Simulation Training Data Set: Puts, N = 3991)

Equation	a	bM	bt	bs	R^2
$D = a + bM + e$	0.004652	0.854840			0.02685
	(0.805)	(0.831)			
$D = a + bt + e$	0.035485		-0.083609		0.47090
	(4.694)		(-4.717)		
$D = a + bs + e$	0.232705			-1.083688	0.08325
	(1.544)			(-1.507)	

Source: Reprinted by permission of the *Journal of Computational Intelligence in Finance*, February/March 1998, © 1998, Finance and Technology Publishing.

Note: $D = P_{GANN} - P_S$ (or neural network put price - target put price), M = degree of moneyness ($F(t) - (100 - K)$), t = time to maturity, and s = volatility measure.

The terms a and b are the regression coefficients and e is the error term.

All t-statistics are below their respective coefficients in parentheses.

Validation Sample

The trained GANNs were presented with new data in order to test the neural network's ability to approximate simulated put option prices out-of-sample. The results of the GANNs ability to accurately price put options in the validation data set are presented in Table 4.10. In this table, all variables are as previously described, and the data set is divided into sub-samples based on the degree of moneyness.

The results for the entire sample (36,412 observations) indicate a MSE and MAE of 0.00023 and 0.01129 respectively. These errors are similar to those found in the training data set (MSE = 0.00022 and MAE = 0.01083). There were 17,806 in-the-money puts and this category had a MSE of 0.00021 and a MAE of 0.01068. For all out-of-the-money puts (18,408 observations), the MSE and MAE are 0.00024 and 0.01179, while for all at-the-money puts (198 observations) the MSE and MAE are 0.00066 and 0.02025.

Table 4.10: Results Of Genetic Adaptive Neural Network (GANN) Approximation Of The Chen & Scott Modified Black-Scholes Formula (BS$_{CS}$ OPM) (Simulation Validation Data Set: Puts)

Sub-sample Description	Number of Observations	Mean Squared Error (MSE)	Mean Absolute Error (MAE)
Complete Sample	36412	0.00023	0.01129
$M^* > .01$	17806	0.00021	0.01068
$.01 < M < 1.5$	11432	0.00023	0.01169
$M > 1.5$	6374	0.00017	0.00889
$M < -.01$	18408	0.00024	0.01179
$-1.5 < M < -.01$	11972	0.00025	0.01185
$M < -1.5$	6436	0.00023	0.01167
$-.01 < M < .01$	198	0.00066	0.02025

* M is a measure of the degree of moneyness. For example, if the futures rate ($F(t)$) is greater than the strike rate ($100 - K$), a put option on a 3-month Eurodollar futures contract will be in-the-money. Therefore, M is defined as $F(t) - (100 - K)$, and when $M > .01$ the put option is in-the-money.

Upon further examination of the in-the-money category, the GANN approximated deep in-the-money puts ($M > 1.5$) better than just in-the-money put options ($0.01 < M < 1.5$). These results are similar to the results for the training data sample and the results found with call options. The MAE for the deep in-the-money category is 0.00889 compared to 0.01169 for the just in-the-money category.

For pricing out-of-the-money puts, the GANN approximated deep out-of-the-money puts ($M < -1.5$) better than just out-of-the-money puts ($-1.5 < M < -.01$) in terms of MSE and MAE. The MAE for deep out-of-the-money puts is 0.01167 as compared to an MAE of 0.01185 for just out-of-the-money puts.

Collectively, the GANN performed well when pricing put options out of sample. The smallest error, as measured by MAE, was found when approximating deep in-the-money puts while the largest error occurred when pricing at-the-money puts. These results are similar to what was found with the training sample for puts and with the analysis for simulated call prices.

Tests for significance on the observed errors were conducted, and the results are presented in Table 4.11. At the .01 level, the hypothesis that $D = 0$ can be rejected for the deep out-of-the-money ($M < -1.5$) and the deep in-the-money ($M > 1.5$) sub-samples when using the paired sample t-test. At the .05 level the hypothesis of equivalence can be rejected for the in-the-money ($M > .01$) category and the complete sample (36,412 observations).

When utilizing the Wilcoxon test, the hypothesis of equivalence between the GANN approximation and the simulated put price can be rejected at the .01 level for the in-the-money ($M > .01$), out-of-the-money ($M < -.01$), just out-of-the-money ($-1.5 < M < -.01$), and deep out-of-the-money ($M < -1.5$) sub-samples. At the .05 level, the hypothesis that $D = 0$ can be rejected for the just in-the-money ($.01 < M < 1.5$) category. There is not sufficient evidence to reject the hypothesis of equivalence for the complete sample (36,412 observations), the deep in-the-money ($M > 1.5$), or the at-the-money ($-.01 < M < .01$) categories.

Table 4.11: Comparison Of Simulation And Genetic Adaptive Neural Network Prices For Put Options (Panel A: Paired Sample t-test, Validation Sample)

Sub-sample Description	Number of Observations	Average Simulation Price (P$_S$)	Average GANN Price (P$_{GANN}$)	Mean D*	t-value	2-tailed Significance
Complete Sample	36412	0.6402	0.6400	-0.0002	-2.56	0.011
M** > .01	17806	1.2513	1.2511	-0.0002	-2.13	0.033
.01 < M < 1.5	11432	0.8020	0.8022	0.0002	1.35	0.177
M > 1.5	6374	2.0572	2.0562	-0.0010	-6.05	0.000
M < -.01	18408	0.0532	0.0530	-0.0002	-1.69	0.091
-1.5 < M < -.01	11972	0.0800	0.0801	0.0002	1.07	0.285
M < -1.5	6436	0.0033	0.0025	-0.0008	-4.52	0.000
-.01 < M < .01	198	0.2581	0.2598	0.0016	0.90	0.368

Table 4.11 (continued)

Sub-sample Description	Number of Observations	Mean - Rank	Mean + Rank	Cases-Ranks/+ Ranks	Z-value	2-tailed Significance
Complete Sample	36412	17970.11	18444.42	18531/17874	-0.8301	0.4065
$M** > .01$	17806	9097.76	8724.96	8454/9349	-3.3959	0.0007
$.01 < M < 1.5$	11432	5979.58	5486.53	5320/6111	-2.4330	0.0150
$M > 1.5$	6374	3181.25	3191.58	3134/3238	-1.2403	0.2149
$M < -.01$	18408	8723.00	9770.00	9976/8428	-3.2463	0.0012
$-1.5 < M < -.01$	11972	5644.13	6464.19	6994/4975	-9.6763	0.0000
$M < -1.5$	6436	3114.79	3307.13	2982/3453	-7.1501	0.0000
$-.01 < M < .01$	198	103.89	94.93	101/97	-0.7952	0.4265

Source: Reprinted by permission of the *Journal of Computational Intelligence in Finance*, February/March 1998, © 1998, Finance and Technology Publishing.

* D = Average difference in predicted value from actual value ($P_{GANN} - P_S$), ** M = degree of moneyness ($F(t) - (100 - K)$). The term -*Ranks* refers to cases where $P_S > P_{GANN}$, while +*Ranks* refers to cases where $P_S < P_{GANN}$.

Altogether, the evidence suggests that the GANN had some difficulties pricing out-of-the-money puts. The hypothesis that D = 0 can be rejected for the case of deep out-of-the-money puts and perhaps for the just out-of-the-money and out-of-the money categories. Although not conclusive, the results indicate that the GANN approximation is not significantly different from the simulated put price for the complete sample and for many of the sub-samples. Furthermore, though a number of sub-samples have a significant *D* variable, the magnitudes of the errors are small as measure by *D*, *MSE*, and *MAE*.

As with the previous samples, regressions were conducted on the degree of moneyness, time to expiration, and the volatility of the underlying futures rate in order to test for pricing biases. The OLS regression results are presented in Table 4.12. None of the explanatory variable are significant at the .01 level. At the .05 level, the maturity coefficient is significant. This indicates the possibility of a maturity bias in the GANN put option price approximations. The coefficient is negative, as it was with the training sample, suggesting that the GANN tends to underprice put options with longer maturities.

In summarizing the results for the put option pricing simulation, the evidence is insufficient to refute the hypothesis that *D* = 0 with the exception of out-of-the-money puts. Thus, the GANN has been able to accurately approximate the simulated put option prices. This is similar to the results with the simulated call option prices. Also, as with the call options, statistically significant differences can be found in some sub-samples, but the differences are not significant for the sample as a whole, nor are they significant for all of the sub-samples. Although there may be a pricing bias with respect to maturity, the magnitudes of the errors are small. The MAE is close to .01 for all sub-samples with the exception of the at-the-money category. Altogether, the results support the notion that the GANN was able to approximate the underlying function that was used to generate the simulated put option prices.

Table 4.12: OLS Regression Results Of Pricing Errors On Selected Parameters (Validation Training Data Set: Puts, N = 36412)

Equation	a	bM	bt	bs	R^2
$D = a + bM + e$	-2.068E-04	-9.778E-05			0.00009
	(-2.603)	(-1.788)			
$D = a + bt + e$	-5.218E-04		7.739E-04		0.00012
	(-3.008)		(2.066)		
$D = a + bs + e$	-0.001038			0.004001	0.00000
	(-0.430)			(0.345)	

Note: $D = P_{GANN} - P_S$ (or neural network put price - target put price), M = degree of moneyness $(F(t) - (100 - K))$, t = time to maturity, and s = volatility measure.

The terms a and b are the regression coefficients and e is the error term.

All t-statistics are below their respective coefficients in parentheses.

SENSITIVITY ANALYSIS

Although neural networks have been found to provide superior performance to other techniques for classification and approximations purposes, they are frequently criticized because the internal structure of the model is unknown. Without knowing the internal structure, users can only inspect the output of the network and hope that the neural network produces a logical output for the inputs provided. Altman et al. (1994) found "illogical weightings of the indicators" when comparing neural networks to Multiple Discriminant Analysis and Logit in predicting corporate distress. In one case, he found that if a firm's liquidity position worsened, the neural network output showed a decreased likelihood of financial distress. This is exactly the opposite of what one would expect. In some instances, the improvement in the firm's position was large enough to move what was an unsound firm into the category of healthy firms.

In light of Altman's findings, and in light of the fact that the neural network's internal structure is unknown, a sensitivity analysis of the inputs is a necessary step in a study utilizing neural networks. For this study, a sensitivity analysis was conducted on the four inputs, the futures rate $(F(t))$, the strike rate $(100 - K)$, the time to maturity (t), and the volatility (s). In conducting a sensitivity analysis, one input variable is allowed to change while all other input variables are held constant. The effect of the change in that one variable on the output variable is then recorded.

In examining the effect of a change in the futures rate on the GANN approximation for call and put values, the strike price was set at 95 (alternatively, the strike rate was 5), the time to maturity at 0.412, and volatility at 0.209. These values are the means for those inputs from the simulation data set. The futures rate was allowed to vary from 3.139 to 6.316 (the minimum and maximum values from the simulation data set) in increments of approximately 0.064 to yield 50 observations. Recall from the previous chapter that an increase in the futures rate implies a decrease in the futures price. As the futures rate increases (futures price decreases) the value of a call option on that futures will decrease and the value of a put option will increase. This implies an indirect relationship between the futures rate and a call value and a direct relationship between the futures rate and a put value. Plots of the

GANN's approximations and the simulated call and put option prices are shown in Figure 4.1 and Figure 4.2, respectively.

In reviewing Figure 4.1, it is clear that the GANN has arrived at a "logical weighting" for the futures rate input variable. An increase in the futures rate leads to a decrease in the GANN call price approximation. Further, as shown in Figure 4.2, the GANN put price approximation is an increasing function of the futures rate.

There is a direct relationship between the strike rate, $(100 - K)$, and the value of a call. A small strike rate (or a large strike price) means that the futures price must rise significantly (futures rate must fall significantly) to be in-the-money. Therefore, a small strike rate corresponds to a small call value. There is an indirect relationship between the strike rate and the value of a put option. Plots of the GANN's call and put approximations are shown in Figures 4.3 and 4.4.

In examining the GANN's call and put approximations, the futures rate was set at 5, the time to maturity at 0.412, and volatility at 0.209. The strike rate was allowed to vary from 3 to 7 in steps of .08. The plots show the GANN call approximation as an increasing function of the strike rate and the GANN put approximation as a decreasing function of the strike rate. These relationships are as they should be, so it appears that the GANN has derived logical weightings for the strike rate variable.

There is a direct relationship between the price of a call and the time to maturity. When there is a long time to maturity, there is a greater probability of a larger futures price and, therefore, a larger call price. A longer time to expiration also gives a put option more time to increase in value. This implies a positive relationship between the time to maturity and option value for both calls and puts.

The GANN's approximations of call and put prices for different maturities are shown in Figures 4.5 and 4.6. In creating the plots, the futures rate was set at 5, the strike price at 95 (strike rate at 5), and the volatility at 0.209. Thus, the plots are for at-the-money call and put options. The plots show the GANN approximations as increasing functions of the time to expiration. Recall that the largest errors (as measured by MAE) were reported for the GANN's approximations of at-the-money calls and puts. This is evidenced by the difference in the simulation prices and neural network approximations in Figures 4.5 and 4.6. Looking back at the sensitivity plots for the futures rate and strike

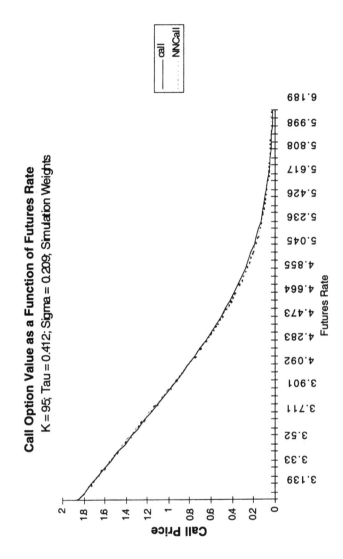

Figure 4. 1

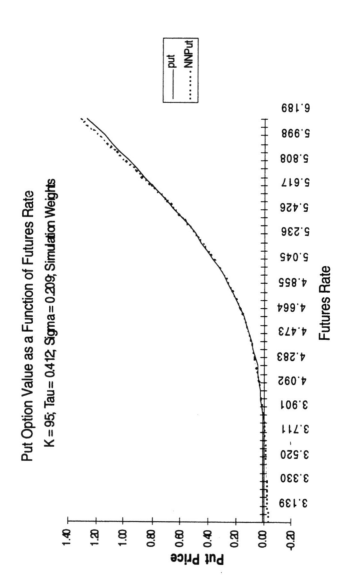

Figure 4. 2

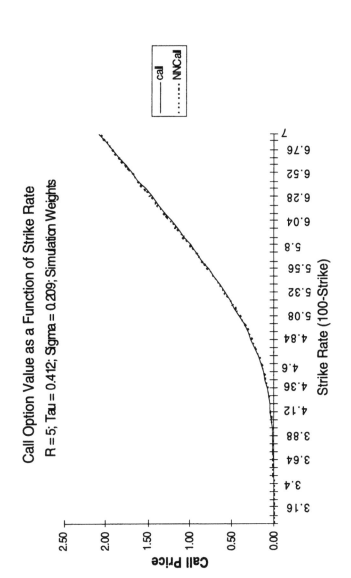

Call Option Value as a Function of Strike Rate

R = 5; Tau = 0.412; Sigma = 0.209; Simulation Weights

Figure 4. 3

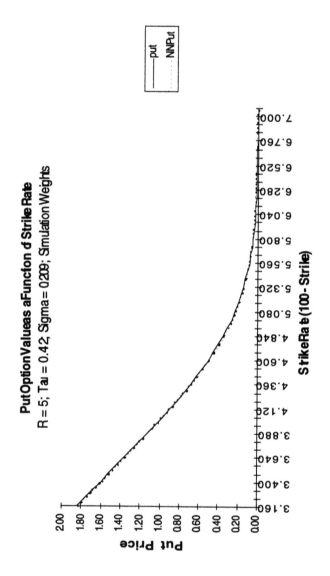

Figure 4. 4

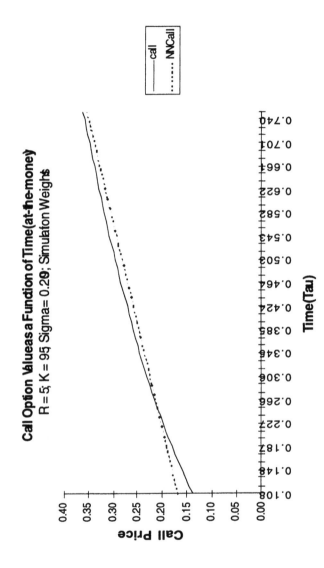

Call Option Value as a Function of Time (at-the-money)
R = 5; K = 95 Sigma = 0.29; Simulation Weights

Call Price

0.40
0.35
0.30
0.25
0.20
0.15
0.10
0.05
0.00

Time (Tau)

0.108
0.148
0.182
0.227
0.266
0.306
0.346
0.385
0.424
0.462
0.503
0.543
0.582
0.622
0.661
0.701
0.740

— call
······ NNCall

Figure 4. 5

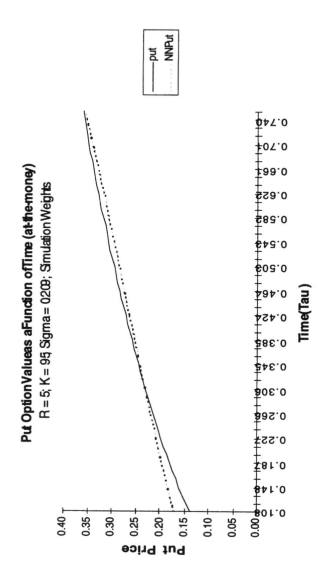

Put Option Values a Function of Time (at-the-money)
R = 5; K = 95; Sigma = 0.209; Simulation Weights

put
NNPut

Put Price

Time (Tau)

Figure 4. 6

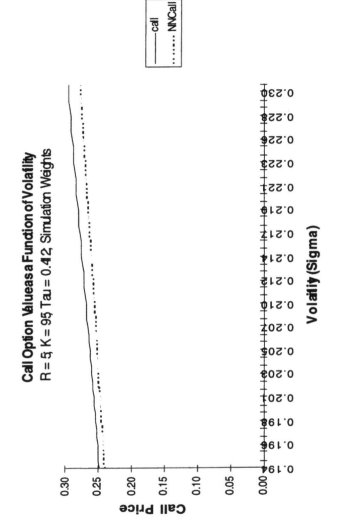

Figure 4.7

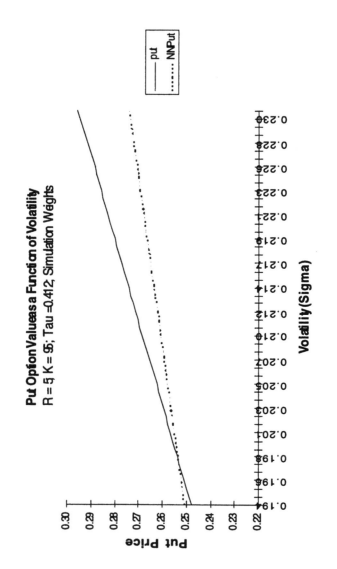

Figure 4. 8

rate, the GANN approximations tracked much closer to the simulated call and put price.

As with time to maturity, there is a direct relationship between the price of a call and the futures' volatility. With a larger volatility, the probability of a higher futures price (lower futures rate) is greater and so is the value of a call. An increase in volatility will affect a put in the same way as a call. A larger volatility means a larger range of prices which increases the probability that the futures' price will be below the exercise price at expiration, thereby increasing the value of the put.

The GANN approximations as a function of volatility are shown in Figures 4.7 and 4.8. As with time to maturity, at-the-money options ($R = 5$, $100 - K = 5$) were examined and the time to maturity was set at 0.412. Also, as with the previous inputs, the variable being examined was allowed to increase from its minimum to its maximum simulation value in equivalent increments. Review of Figure 4.7 and Figure 4.8 show that the GANN approximations are increasing functions of volatility. Again, the larger pricing errors for at-the-money options show up in the plots.

The sensitivity plots plainly show that the GANN has arrived at logical weightings for all of the input variables. Although some studies have found illogical weightings, these studies have almost exclusively utilized a back-propagation neural network (BPNN). As mentioned in the previous chapter, one of the shortcomings of BPNNs is their tendency to become stuck at local, rather than global, optima. Because the GANN is an intelligent global search technique, the problem of arriving at local optima is addressed here.

In concluding this section, the GANN's ability to approximate a complex, non-linear option pricing model has been tested. The results indicate that the GANN is indeed able to approximate the call and put option prices produced by the aforementioned option pricing model. The differences in the GANNs call and put price approximations were not found to be significantly different from the simulation prices for the sample as a whole. This was also true for many of the sub-samples examined. Although the pricing errors in some sub-samples were statistically significant, the errors were relatively small as measured by MAE. Finally, an examination of the input variables showed that the GANN arrived at logical weightings when trained on the simulated data set.

SECTION II: REAL DATA RESULTS

In this section, the GANNs ability to accurately approximate options on 3-month Eurodollar futures is presented. As was described in the previous chapter, a number of training and holdout data sets were drawn, covering the period January 4, 1994 through July 29, 1994. From this data, a training set was constructed that consisted of 2,000 observations randomly selected from the period January 4, 1994 through June 9, 1994. The remaining 6887 observations were used to construct a holdout sample, HOLDOUT 1. To test the trained GANNs ability to approximate options outside the training set, four additional validation samples were constructed, each one representing a week in July 1994.

As with the simulation data, a separate GANN was developed for call and put options. The inputs for each were the futures rate $F(t)$, the strike rate $(100 - K)$, the annualized volatility of the underlying futures contract (u), and time to maturity (t). Also, as with the simulation data, a number of network topologies were tested. All of the networks tested had one input layer consisting of four (4) input nodes, one hidden layer, and one output layer consisting of one node. Ultimately, based on minimizing MSE, it was determined that the neural networks which provided superior performance for this particular data set were those with 18 hidden layer nodes. The networks were trained until no further improvement in SSE was obtained, then they were trained an additional 30,000 generations in a fine-tuning process. After training, the GANNs results were compared to the actual option prices and to the BS_{CS} OPM approximation.

Call Options

The results of the GANNs ability to approximate call options traded on the 3-month Eurodollar futures contract are presented in Table 4.13. MSEs and MAEs are reported for both the GANN approximation and the BS_{CS} OPM approximation. Error terms were calculated as the neural network predicted call price (C_{GANN}) minus the target price (the market price, C) or as the BS_{CS} predicted price (C_{BS}) minus the target price. As with the previous section, the data is divided into a number of sub-samples based on the degree of moneyness. Unlike the last section, however, a call option was determined to be deep in-the-money or deep out-of-the-money if M > 1 or M < -1, respectively. The different parameter was necessary in order to keep the sample sized large for those categories.

The results for the entire training sample (2000 observations) indicate a MSE and MAE of 0.00047 and 0.01589 for the GANN and 0.02012 and 0.07743 for the BS_{CS} OPM. Recall, from the previous chapter, that the minimum size tick-move for the 3-month Eurodollar futures option is .01. This means that the average pricing error from the GANN is almost as small as the minimum price move allowed by LIFFE. The average error for the BS_{CS} OPM is seven (7) times the minimum tick move.

Both models performed best when approximating out-of-the-money ($M < -.01$) and deep out-of-the-money ($M < -1$) options and worst when approximating the at-the-money category ($-.01 < M < .01$). This is true for both the training sample and the holdout sample (6887 observations). The errors are smaller for the GANN than for the BS_{CS} OPM for all the sub-samples. For most of the sub-samples, the BS_{CS} MAE is larger than the GANN MAE by a factor of 5. This implies that the average error for the BS_{CS} OPM is five times the average error for the GANN.

Both paired t-tests and Wilcoxon signed-ranks tests were employed to determine if the observed differences were significant. The hypotheses tested were:

HA_0: The GANN call option price is the same as the market call option price. Alternatively, $C_{GANN} - C = 0$.

HA_1: The GANN call option price is not the same as the market call option price. Alternatively, $C_{GANN} - C = 0$.

and

HB_0: The error produced by the GANN approximation is greater than or equal to the error produced by the BS_{CS} OPM approximation. Alternatively, $C_{GANN} - C \geq C_{BS} - C$.

HB_1: The error produced by the GANN approximation is less than the error produced by the BS_{CS} OPM approximation. Alternatively, $C_{GANN} - C < C_{BS} - C$.

Table 4.13: Results Of Genetic Adaptive Neural Network (GANN) Approximation Of Eurodollar Call Futures Option Traded On LIFFE (Panel B: Training Data Set)

Sub-sample Description	Number of Observations	BSCS OPM Approximation		GANN Approximation	
		Mean Squared Error (MSE)	Mean Absolute Error (MAE)	Mean Squared Error (MSE)	Mean Absolute Error (MAE)
Complete Sample	2000	0.02012	0.07743	0.00047	0.01589
$M^* > .01$	790	0.02939	0.10903	0.00066	0.02012
$.01 < M < 1$	517	0.03381	0.11526	0.00072	0.02083
$M > 1$	271	0.02116	0.09785	0.00055	0.01871
$M < -.01$	1202	0.01348	0.05568	0.00033	0.01306
$-1 < M < -.01$	577	0.02641	0.09886	0.00048	0.01597
$M < -1$	619	0.00155	0.01575	0.00019	0.01028
$-.01 < M < .01$	8	0.10399	0.22549	0.00140	0.02345

Table 4.13 (continued)

Sub-sample Description	Number of Observations	BSCS OPM Approximation		GANN Approximation	
		Mean Squared Error (MSE)	Mean Absolute Error (MAE)	Mean Squared Error (MSE)	Mean Absolute Error (MAE)
Complete Sample	6887	0.01759	0.07162	0.00051	0.01677
$M^* > .01$	2698	0.02822	0.10593	0.00071	0.02098
$.01 < M < 1$	1782	0.03290	0.11229	0.00076	0.02159
$M > 1$	910	0.01912	0.09361	0.00061	0.01978
$M < -.01$	4159	0.01051	0.04892	0.00038	0.01399
$-1 < M < -.01$	1840	0.02174	0.09017	0.00059	0.01722
$M < -1$	2312	0.00159	0.01608	0.00022	0.01143
$-.01 < M < .01$	30	0.04373	0.13311	0.00117	0.02360

* M is a measure of the degree of moneyness. For example, if the strike rate $(100 - K)$ is greater than the futures rate $(F(t))$, a call option on a 3-month Eurodollar futures contract will be in-the-money. Therefore, M is defined as $(100 - K) - F(t)$, and when $M > .01$ the call option is in-the-money.

Table 4.14: Paired-Comparison T-Test Results Of Eurodollar Call Futures Option Approximation Methods (Panel A: Training Data Set)

Sample Group	N	C_{GANN} vs. Market Price		C_{GANN} vs. C_{BS}	
		t-statistic	p-value	t-statistic	p-value
Complete Sample	2000	0.000	1.000	-28.669	0.000
$M^* > .01$	790	-0.270	0.787	-22.606	0.000
$.01 < M < 1$	517	-0.629	0.530	-17.570	0.000
$M > 1$	271	0.549	0.583	-15.495	0.000
$M < -.01$	1202	0.147	0.883	-18.833	0.000
$-1 < M < -.01$	577	0.580	0.562	18.155	0.000
$M < -1$	619	-0.523	0.601	-11.105	0.000
$-.01 < M < .01$	8	0.969	0.365	-2.256	0.030

Table 4.14 (continued)

Sample Group	N	C_{GANN} vs. Market Price		C_{GANN} vs. C_{BS}	
		t-statistic	p-value	t-statistic	p-value
Complete Sample	6887	1.001	0.317	-52.206	0.000
$M^* > .01$	2698	-0.654	0.513	-41.540	0.000
$.01 < M < 1$	1782	-1.457	0.145	-32.524	0.000
$M > 1$	910	1.027	0.305	-28.400	0.000
$M < -.01$	4159	2.126	0.034	-34.191	0.000
$-1 < M < -.01$	1840	1.899	0.058	-32.327	0.000
$M < -1$	2312	0.888	0.375	-20.335	0.000
$-.01 < M < .01$	30	0.609	0.547	-4.104	0.000

* M is a measure of the degree of moneyness, C_{GANN} and C_{BS} are the Genetic Adaptive Neural Network and Chen & Scott (1993) approximations, respectively. When comparing C_{GANN} to the market price, the p-value is for a 2-tailed test. When comparing C_{GANN} to C_{BS}, the p-value is for a 1-tailed test.

Hypothesis A is similar to the hypothesis tested in the previous section while Hypothesis B tests whether the observed differences in errors from the two approximation techniques are significant.

Results from the paired-comparison t-tests are presented in Table 4.14. Hypothesis A cannot be rejected at the .01 level for any of the sub-samples in the training data set or in the holdout set. At the .05 level, the hypothesis of equivalence between the GANN approximation and the market price can only be rejected for the out-of-the-money category in the holdout sample. Hypothesis B is rejected at the .01 level for all but one category, at-the-money calls in the training sample. At the .05 level, the hypothesis that the GANN errors are greater than or equal to the BS_{CS} OPM errors is rejected for every sub-sample in both the training and holdout data sets.

The Wilcoxon signed-ranks test results are presented in Table 4.15. Conducting non-parametric tests was appropriate, as the approximation errors appeared to be non-normally distributed. At the .05 level for the training data set, there is insufficient evidence to reject Hypothesis A for any sub-sample and Hypothesis B is rejected at every sub-sample. This is true at the .01 level also, with the exception of the at-the-money category, in which Hypothesis B is rejected. For the holdout sample, the hypothesis of equivalence between the GANN approximation and the market price is rejected for the deep out-of-the-money, out-of-the-money and complete sample categories. At the .05 level, Hypothesis A is rejected for the deep in-the-money and just out-of-the-money categories. Hypothesis B is strongly rejected for all sub-samples which implies that the errors produced by the GANN approximation are smaller than the errors produced by the BS_{CS} approximation.

To gain further insights into the performance of the models, OLS regressions are utilized to test for the existence of pricing biases. The regression results from these tests are presented in Table 4.16. In examining the BS_{CS} OPM, the existence of pricing biases with respect to degree of moneyness, time to maturity, and volatility is confirmed. The model with volatility (u) as the explanatory variable has the highest R^2, and the model with time to maturity (t) as the explanatory variable has the smallest R^2. For the GANN, the existence of pricing biases cannot be confirmed at the .01 level for the training sample, nor the holdout sample.

Table 4.15: Wilcoxon Signed-Ranks Test Results Of Eurodollar Call Futures Option Approximation Methods (Panel A: Training Data Set)

Sample Group	N	C_{GANN} vs. Market Price		C_{GANN} vs. C_{BS}	
		Z-value	p-value	Z-value	p-value
Complete Sample	2000	-0.591	0.555	-33.682	0.000
$M^* > .01$	790	-0.151	0.880	-22.476	0.000
$.01 < M < 1$	517	-1.194	0.232	-18.494	0.000
$M > 1$	271	-1.467	0.142	-12.573	0.000
$M < -.01$	1202	-1.147	0.251	-24.828	0.000
$-1 < M < -.01$	577	-0.773	0.440	-19.790	0.000
$M < -1$	619	-0.947	0.343	-13.138	0.000
$-.01 < M < .01$	8	-0.280	0.779	-2.100	0.018

Table 4.15 (continued)

Sample Group	N	C_{GANN} vs. Market Price		C_{GANN} vs. C_{BS}	
		Z-value	p-value	Z-value	p-value
Complete Sample	6887	-3.305	0.001	-61.054	0.000
$M^* > .01$	2698	-0.611	0.541	-41.830	0.000
$.01 < M < 1$	1782	-1.126	0.260	-34.768	0.000
$M > 1$	910	-2.517	0.012	-22.889	0.000
$M < -.01$	4159	-4.137	0.000	-43.272	0.000
$-1 < M < -.01$	1840	-2.157	0.031	-34.445	0.000
$M < -1$	2312	-3.666	0.000	-23.084	0.000
$-.01 < M < .01$	30	-0.051	0.959	-4.247	0.000

* M is a measure of the degree of moneyness, C_{GANN} and C_{BS} are the Genetic Adaptive Neural Network and Chen & Scott (1993) approximations, respectively. When comparing C_{GANN} to the market price, the p-value is for a 2-tailed test. When comparing C_{GANN} to C_{BS}, the p-value is for a 1-tailed test.

Altogether, the evidence for call options is straightforward. The pricing errors produced by the GANN are not significantly different from zero with the exception of the out-of-the-money, deep out-of-the-money and perhaps overall sub-samples. Further, the errors produced by the GANN are smaller (as measured by MSE and MAE) than those produced by the BSCS OPM. The evidence supports the hypothesis that the GANN errors are significantly smaller than the BSCS OPM errors. Finally, the BSCS OPM appears to produce pricing biases related to the degree of moneyness, the time to maturity and the volatility of the underlying futures contract. Such spurious relationships were not found with the GANN call approximations.

Those familiar with options applications may point out that this study is comparing the Genetic Adaptive Neural Network to a "naUive" option pricing model. Here the term naïve refers to the fact that historical volatility was used as the volatility estimate in the BS_{CS}OPM. As many of the aforementioned problems with traditional option pricing models have been well documented, including the reliability of the assumption of constant volatility and the pricing biases that exist, most practitiones use a "calibrated" option pricing model.

In practice, the model is calibrated by constructing a volatility matrix using implied volatilities. Implied volatilities are determined from observed market option prices aof at-the-money options of various maturities. These implied volatilities are then used in the option pricing models (as opposed to annualized historical volatilities) to value in-the-money or out-of-the-money options. A recent expansion of this study by White, Hatfield and Dorsey (1998) compared GANN to a BS_{CS}OPM calibrated in the same manner as LIFFE calibrates their model. The GANN was still found to significantly outperform the traditional OPM by producing pricing errors that are 2 to 3 times smaller than the BS_{CS}OPM.

PUT OPTIONS

To test the GANN's ability to approximate put prices on the 3-month Eurodollar futures option traded on LIFFE, a neural network consisting of four (4) input nodes, eighteen (18) hidden layer nodes and one output node was developed and trained on the 2000 observation training data set. As with call options, when this network's training was completed, it was presented with the 6887 observation holdout data set

Table 4.16: OLS Regression Results Of Eurodollar Call Futures Options Pricing Errors On Selected Parameters (Panel A: Training Data Set GANN Results, N = 2000)

Equation	a	bM	bt	bu	R^2
$D = a + bM + e$	-2.7E-08 (0.000)	-7.6E-.08 (0.000)			0.000
$D = a + bt + e$	-1.4E-07 (0.000)		3.0E-07 (0.000)		0.000
$D = a + bu + e$	-2.7E-07 (0.000)			8.4E-.07 (0.000)	0.000
(Panel B: Training Data Set BSCS OPM Results, N = 2000)					
$D = a + bM + e$	0.088 (33.183)	0.029 (13.883)			0.088
$D = a + bt + e$	0.059 (11.217)		0.038 (3.980)		0.008
$D = a + bu + e$	-0.141 (-45.059)			0.683 (77.258)	0.749

Table 4.16 (continued)

(Panel C: HOLDOUT1 GANN Results, N = 6887)

Model	a	bM	bt	bu	R^2
$D = a + bM + e$	1.5E-04 (0.517)	-2.9E-04 (-1.322)			0.000
$D = a + bt + e$	1.2E-03 (2.111)		-1.8E-03 (-1.859)		0.001
$D = a + bu + e$	5.0E-05 (0.078)			7.0E-04 (0.379)	0.000

(Panel D: HOLDOUT1 BSCS OPM Results, N = 6887)

Model	a	bM	bt	bu	R^2
$D = a + bM + e$	0.084 (61.752)	0.028 (27.298)			0.098
$D = a + bt + e$	0.054 (19.996)		0.038 (7.723)		0.009
$D = a + bu + e$	-0.132 (-77.174)			0.642 (131.264)	0.714

Note: $D = C_{GANN}$ - C (or neural network call price - market call price) for the panels that relate to GANN and $D = C_{BS}$ - C for the panels that apply to the BSCS OPM. M = degree of moneyness $((100 - K) - F(t))$, t = time to maturity, and u = volatility measure.

The terms a and b are the regression coefficients and e is the error term.

All t-statistics are below their respective coefficients in parentheses.

(HOLDOUT1). Put price approximations were also calculated with the BS_{CS} OPM for both data sets. Error terms were calculated as the approximation price minus the actual market price for both models ($P_{GANN} - P$ and $P_{BS} - P$ for the GANN and the BS_{CS} OPM respectively). MSEs and MAEs are presented in Table 4.17.

For the entire training data set (2000 observations) the GANN's MSE and MAE are 0.00044 and 0.01598 as compared to 0.02012 and 0.07743 for the BS_{CS} OPM. These numbers are similar to those reported for call options. Both the GANN and the BS_{CS} OPM produced the smallest errors (as measured by MAE) in the deep in-the-money (M > 1) category. The GANN also had small errors in the deep out-of-the-money (M < -1) and the in-the-money (M > .01) training sample categories. The BS_{CS} OPM's next smallest errors were recorded in the in-the-money category. The largest errors for both models were in the at-the-money sub-sample (-.01 < M < .01).

For the holdout sample, the largest error for both models were in the at-the-money sub-sample. The smallest errors for both models were in the in-the-money and deep in-the-money sub-samples. The errors are smaller for the GANN than for the BS_{CS} OPM in all sub-samples and, as measured by MAE, are often smaller by a factor of 5 or more. The smallest difference in MAE for the two models occurred in the deep in-the-money category. For this sub-sample the MAE was 0.0157 and 0.01377 in the training data set and 0.01608 and 0.01328 in the holdout sample for the GANN and the BS_{CS} OPM, respectively.

In order to gain further insights on the observed pricing errors, both paired comparison t-tests and Wilcoxon signed-ranks tests were employed to determine if the errors were significant. Once again, examination of the errors indicated the possibility of non-normality, necessitating the use of non-parametric tests. The hypotheses tested were:

HA_0: The GANN put option price is the same as the market put price. Alternatively, $P_{GANN} - P = 0$.

HA_1: The GANN put option price is not the same as the market put price. Alternatively, $P_{GANN} - P = 0$.

and,

Table 4.17: Results Of Genetic Adaptive Neural Network (GANN) Approximation Of Eurodollar Put Futures Option Traded On LIFFE (Panel A: Training Data Set)

Sub-sample Description	Number of Observations	BSCS OPM Approximation		GANN Approximation	
		Mean Squared Error (MSE)	Mean Absolute Error (MAE)	Mean Squared Error (MSE)	Mean Absolute Error (MAE)
Complete Sample	2000	0.02012	0.07743	0.00044	0.01598
$M^* > .01$	1202	0.01348	0.05568	0.00039	0.01511
$.01 < M < 1$	577	0.02641	0.09886	0.00047	0.01648
$M > 1$	619	0.00155	0.01575	0.00031	0.01377
$M < -.01$	790	0.02939	0.10903	0.00051	0.01726
$-1 < M < -.01$	517	0.03381	0.11526	0.00061	0.01872
$M < -1$	271	0.02116	0.09785	0.00032	0.01442
$-.01 < M < .01$	8	0.10399	0.22549	0.00129	0.02194

Table 4.17 (continued)

(Panel B: Holdout Data Set, HOLDOUT1)

Sub-sample Description	Number of Observations	BSCS OPM Approximation		GANN Approximation	
		Mean Squared Error (MSE)	Mean Absolute Error (MAE)	Mean Squared Error (MSE)	Mean Absolute Error (MAE)
Complete Sample	6887	0.01759	0.07162	0.00046	0.01632
$M^* > .01$	4159	0.01051	0.04892	0.00041	0.01511
$.01 < M < 1$	1840	0.02174	0.09017	0.00056	0.01740
$M > 1$	2312	0.00159	0.01608	0.00029	0.01328
$M < -.01$	2698	0.02822	0.10593	0.00054	0.01806
$-1 < M < -.01$	1782	0.03290	0.11229	0.00062	0.01898
$M < -1$	910	0.01912	0.09361	0.00039	0.01627
$-.01 < M < .01$	30	0.04373	0.13312	0.00118	0.02606

* M is a measure of the degree of moneyness. For example, if the futures rate ($F(t)$) is greater than the strike rate ($100 - K$), a put option on a 3-month Eurodollar futures contract will be in-the-money. Therefore, M is defined as $F(t) - (100 - K)$, and when $M > .01$ the put option is in-the-money.

HB$_0$: The error produced by the GANN approximation is greater than or equal to the error produced by the BS$_{CS}$ OPM approximation. Alternatively, $P_{GANN} - P \geq P_{BS} - P$.

HB$_1$: The error produced by the GANN approximation is smaller than the error produced by the BS$_{CS}$ OPM approximation. Alternatively, $P_{GANN} - P < P_{BS} - P$.

Hypothesis A is used to determine if the GANN approximation is significantly different from the market put price while Hypothesis B is used to determine if the GANN is a "better" (in terms of smallest error produced) approximator of market prices than the BS$_{CS}$ OPM.

Results from the paired-comparison t-tests are presented in Table 4.18. At the .01 level, the hypothesis of equivalence between the GANN approximation and the market price (Hypothesis A) can be rejected only for the just in-the-money (.01 < M < 1) category for the training sample. For the holdout sample, Hypothesis A can be rejected at the .01 level for the just in-the-money and the deep in-the-money (M > 1) sub-samples only. Hypothesis A can be rejected for the deep in-the-money category at the .05 level in the training sample.

Hypothesis B is rejected at the .01 level for every sub-sample in the holdout set. In the training set, Hypothesis B is rejected at the .01 level for every sub-sample except the at-the-money (-.01 < M < .01) category. The hypothesis is rejected for this category at the .05 level however. This is compelling evidence that the GANN is indeed a better approximator of put prices than the BS$_{CS}$ OPM.

The results for the Wilcoxon signed-ranks tests are presented in Table 4.19. Hypothesis A can only be rejected at the .01 level for the just in-the-money (.01 < M < 1) training sample category. For the holdout sample, the hypothesis of equivalence can be rejected at the .01 level for the in-the-money (M > .01) and the just in-the-money categories only. At the .05 level, Hypothesis A can be rejected for the deep in-the-money (M > 1) holdout category only. This is further evidence that the GANN approximation is not significantly different from the actual market put price.

Table 4.18: Paired-Comparison T-Test Results Of Eurodollar Put Futures Option Approximation Methods (Panel A: Training Data Set)

Sample Group	N	P_{GANN} vs. Market Price		P_{GANN} vs. P_{BS}	
		t-statistic	p-value	t-statistic	p-value
Complete Sample	2000	0.000	1.000	28.854	0.000
$M^* > .01$	1202	-0.948	0.343	18.801	0.000
$.01 < M < 1$	577	-3.473	0.001	18.795	0.000
$M > 1$	619	2.530	0.012	9.677	0.000
$M < -.01$	790	0.828	0.408	22.880	0.000
$-1 < M < -.01$	517	1.122	0.262	17.828	0.000
$M < -1$	271	-0.258	0.796	15.277	0.000
$-.01 < M < .01$	8	1.215	0.264	2.307	0.027

Table 4.18 (continued)

(Panel B: Holdout Data Set, HOLDOUT1)

Sample Group	N	PGANN vs. Market Price		PGANN vs. PBS	
		t-statistic	p-value	t-statistic	p-value
Complete Sample	6887	-0.796	0.426	52.931	0.000
$M^* > .01$	4159	-1.704	0.088	34.451	0.000
$.01 < M < 1$	1840	-5.953	0.000	33.707	0.000
$M > 1$	2312	4.535	0.000	18.699	0.000
$M < -.01$	2698	0.579	0.563	42.215	0.000
$-1 < M < -.01$	1782	0.973	0.331	32.977	0.000
$M < -1$	910	-0.593	0.553	28.613	0.000
$-.01 < M < .01$	30	0.490	0.628	4.231	0.000

* M is a measure of the degree of moneyness, PGANN and PBS are the Genetic Adaptive Neural Network and Chen & Scott (1993) approximations, respectively. When comparing PGANN to the market price, the p-value is for a 2-tailed test. When comparing PGANN to PBS, the p-value is for a 1-tailed test.

Table 4.19: Wilcoxon Signed-Ranks Test Results Of Eurodollar Put Futures Option Approximation Methods (Panel A: Training Data Set)

Sample Group	N	P$_{GANN}$ vs. Market Price		P$_{GANN}$ vs. P$_{BS}$	
		Z-value	p-value	Z-value	p-value
Complete Sample	2000	-0.585	0.559	-33.657	0.000
$M^* > .01$	1202	-1.831	0.067	-24.803	0.000
$.01 < M < 1$	577	-4.137	0.000	-20.173	0.000
$M > 1$	619	-1.538	0.124	-12.088	0.000
$M < -.01$	790	-1.046	0.296	-22.550	0.000
$-1 < M < -.01$	517	-1.286	0.198	-18.396	0.000
$M < -1$	271	-0.051	0.959	-12.804	0.000
$-.01 < M < .01$	8	-1.540	0.123	-1.960	0.025

Table 4.19 (continued)

(Panel B: Holdout Data Set, HOLDOUT1)

Sample Group	N	PGANN vs. Market Price		PGANN vs. PBS	
		Z-value	p-value	Z-value	p-value
Complete Sample	6887	-1.337	0.181	-62.100	0.000
$M^* > .01$	4159	-3.931	0.000	-44.783	0.000
$.01 < M < 1$	1840	-7.946	0.000	-35.372	0.000
$M > 1$	2312	-2.240	0.025	-23.976	0.000
$M < -.01$	2698	-1.860	0.063	-42.199	0.000
$-1 < M < -.01$	1782	-1.919	0.055	-34.696	0.000
$M < -1$	910	-0.509	0.611	-23.626	0.000
$-.01 < M < .01$	30	-0.031	0.975	-4.309	0.000

* M is a measure of the degree of moneyness, PGANN and PBS are the Genetic Adaptive Neural Network and Chen & Scott (1993) approximations, respectively. When comparing PGANN to the market price, the p-value is for a 2-tailed test. When comparing PGANN to PBS, the p-value is for a 1-tailed test.

Table 4.20: OLS Regression Results Of Eurodollar Put Futures Options Pricing Errors On Selected Parameters (Panel A: Training Data Set GANN Results, N = 2000)

Equation	a	bM	bt	bu	R^2
$D = a + bM + e$	-8.295E-08	-1.155E-07			0.000
	(0.000)	(0.000)			
$D = a + bt + e$	-2.292E-07		2.156E-07		0.000
	(0.000)		(0.000)		
$D = a + bu + e$	-8.312E-07			2.207E-06	0.000
	(-0.001)			(0.0001)	
(Panel B: Training Data Set BSCS OPM Results, N = 2000)					
$D = a + bM + e$	8.845E-02	-2.927E-02			0.088
	(33.183)	(-13.883)			
$D = a + bt + e$	5.915E-02		3.825E-02		0.089
	(11.217)		(3.980)		
$D = a + bu + e$	-0.141			0.683	0.866
	(-45.059)			(77.258)	

Table 4.20 (continued)

(Panel C: HOLDOUT1 GANN Results, N = 6887)

	a	bM	bt	bu	
$D = a + bM + e$	-3.068E-04 (-1.120)	2.378E-04 (1.129)			0.000
$D = a + bt + e$	7.516E-05 (0.145)		-5.897E-04 (-0.627)		0.000
$D = a + bu + e$	-4.682E-04 (-0.761)			8.275E-04 (0.470)	0.000

(Panel D: HOLDOUT1 BSCS OPM Results, N = 6887)

	a	bM	bt	bu	
$D = a + bM + e$	8.352E-02 (61.752)	-2.840E-02 (-27.298)			0.098
$D = a + bt + e$	5.359E-02 (19.996)		3.756E-02 (7.723)		0.009
$D = a + bu + e$	-0.132 (-77.174)			0.642 (131.264)	0.714

Note: $D = P_{GANN} - P$ (or neural network put price - market put price) for the panels that relate to GANN and $D = P_{BS} - P$ for the panels that apply to the BSCS OPM. M = degree of moneyness $(F(t) - (100 - K))$, t = time to maturity, and u = volatility measure.

The terms a and b are the regression coefficients and e is the error term.

All t-statistics are below their respective coefficients in parentheses.

As can be seen from Table 4.19, the errors produced by the GANN are significantly smaller than the pricing errors produced by the BS_{CS} OPM. For the holdout sample, Hypothesis B is rejected at the .01 level for every sub-sample. Furthermore, for the training sample, Hypothesis B is rejected for every sub-sample at the .01 level, except for the at-the-money category which is rejected at the .05 level.

Tests for pricing biases were conducted for the two models tested, the results of which are presented in Table 4.20. For the BS_{CS} OPM, the existence of systematic pricing errors is confirmed for all of the parameters tested in both the training and holdout samples. The regression models with the volatility as the explanatory variable produce the largest R^2 measures. The regression model with time-to-maturity as the dependent variable produces the smallest R^2 in the holdout sample for the BS_{CS} OPM. None of the explanatory variables are significant in any of the regression equations for the GANN. This is true for both the training and holdout data sets. Thus, the results imply that the moneyness bias, the maturity bias and the volatility bias are not present in the GANN but do exist and are confirmed in the BS_{CS} OPM.

Collectively, the evidence for put options is similar to that found with call options. The pricing errors produced by the GANN were not found to be significantly different from zero for most of the sub-samples examined. The errors do appear significant for the in-the-money, just in-the-money and possibly the deep in-the-money categories. Further, the errors produced by the GANN are smaller (as measured by MSE and MAE) than those produced by the BS_{CS} OPM. The evidence supports the hypothesis that the GANN errors are significantly smaller than the BS_{CS} OPM errors. Finally, the BS_{CS} OPM appears to produce pricing biases related to the degree of moneyness, the time to maturity and the volatility of the underlying futures contract. As with call options, such spurious relationships were not found with the GANN put approximations.

ADDITIONAL ANALYSIS OF GANN METHODOLOGIES

One of the advantages of neural networks is there ability to incorporate additional inputs, if necessary, to improve predictive performance. Full advantage of this characteristic of neural networks was not taken by limiting the inputs in the above analysis to just those used by the BS_{CS} OPM. This was necessary however, as the goal was to test the GANN's option pricing abilities using the same inputs as the BS_{CS} OPM. Now that the superior performance of the GANN has been established, new models incorporating additional inputs can be tested.

To test the GANN's ability to incorporate additional economic data, additional neural networks were developed that had six (6) input layer nodes. These inputs were the original four inputs utilized in the original GANNs plus two additional variables. These new variables included a proxy for the degree of moneyness (M), calculated as ($100 - K$) $- F(t)$, and the 3-month Eurodollar (ED) interest rate ($ED03$). The 3-month ED rate was obtained from the Chicago Federal Reserve's on-line market data, available through that bank's World Wide Web page.

The MSEs and MAEs for the new models (denoted $GANN_2$) are presented in Table 4.21. To ease comparison of the new networks with the original networks, the original GANNs results are repeated in this table also (denoted $GANN_1$). To strictly examine the effect of incorporating additional inputs, both GANNs have 18 hidden layer nodes.

As can be seen from Table 4.21, the errors produced by the $GANN_2$ models are often half the size of the errors produced by the $GANN_1$ models. In some sub-samples the MAE is less than the minimum sized price move for the 3-month ED futures options examined. For call options, the MAE is less than .01 (the minimum tick move allowed) for the deep in-the-money, out-of-the-money and deep out-of-the-money sub-samples. For put options, the MAE is less than .01 for in-the-money, deep in-the-money, and deep out-of-the-money options. Thus, the average error produced by the $GANN_2$ models is less than the minimum price move for the above mentioned options. Also, the $GANN_2$ errors (as measured by MSE and MAE) are smaller than the $GANN_1$ errors for both call and puts in all sub-samples.

Table 4.21: Comparison Of Genetic Adaptive Neural Network (GANN) Approximations Of Eurodollar Futures Option Traded On LIFFE (Panel A: Calls)

Sub-sample Description	Number of Observations	GANN$_1$ Approximation		GANN$_2$ Approximation	
		Mean Squared Error (MSE)	Mean Absolute Error (MAE)	Mean Squared Error (MSE)	Mean Absolute Error (MAE)
Complete Sample	6887	0.00051	0.01677	0.00021	0.01018
in-the-money	2698	0.00071	0.02098	0.00028	0.01197
just-in	1782	0.00076	0.02159	0.00036	0.01380
deep-in	910	0.00061	0.01978	0.00014	0.00838
out-of-the-money	4159	0.00038	0.01399	0.00016	0.00898
just-out	1840	0.00059	0.01722	0.00029	0.01251
deep-out	2312	0.00022	0.01143	0.00006	0.00617

Table 4.21 (continued)

(Panel B: Puts)

Sub-sample Description	Number of Observations	GANN$_1$ Approximation		GANN$_2$ Approximation	
		Mean Squared Error (MSE)	Mean Absolute Error (MAE)	Mean Squared Error (MSE)	Mean Absolute Error (MAE)
Complete Sample	6887	0.00046	0.01632	0.00020	0.01014
in-the-money	4159	0.00041	0.01511	0.00016	0.00875
just-in	1840	0.00056	0.01740	0.00029	0.01261
deep-in	2312	0.00029	0.01328	0.00006	0.00566
out-of-the-money	2698	0.00054	0.01806	0.00027	0.01225
just-out	1782	0.00062	0.01898	0.00034	0.01368
deep-out	910	0.00039	0.01627	0.00014	0.00948
at-the-money	30	0.00118	0.02606	0.00036	0.01308

The degree of moneyness is as previously described. For example, if the futures rate ($F(t)$) is greater than the strike rate ($100 - K$), a put option on a 3-month Eurodollar futures contract will be in-the-money and a call option will be out-of-the-money. GANN$_1$ has 4 inputs and 18 hidden layer nodes while GANN$_2$ has 6 input and 18 hidden layer nodes.

Both parametric and non-parametric tests were conducted to determine if the observed error differences were statistically significant. The hypothesis tested was:

H_0:   The average absolute pricing error produced by the $GANN_2$ models are greater than or equal to the average absolute pricing error produced by the $GANN_1$ models. Alternatively, $C_{GANN2} - C \geq C_{GANN1} - C$ and $P_{GANN2} - P \geq P_{GANN1} - P$.

H_1:   The average absolute pricing error produced by the $GANN_2$ models are less the average absolute pricing error produced by the $GANN_1$ models. Alternatively, $C_{GANN2} - C < C_{GANN1} - C$ and $P_{GANN2} - P < P_{GANN1} - P$.

Paired comparison t-tests and Wilcoxon signed-ranks test results are presented in Table 4.22.

In reviewing Table 4.22, it is clear that the observed differences are statistically significant for many of the sub-samples. Utilizing the paired-comparison t-test, at the .05 level, the hypothesis that the $GANN_2$ errors are greater than or equal to the $GANN_1$ errors is rejected for the complete sample (6887 observations) and the deep out-of-the-money categories for calls and for the in-the-money category for puts. At the .01 level, the hypothesis is also rejected for out-of-the-money and just out-of-the-money calls and just in-the-money and deep in-the-money put options.

Based on the Wilcoxon test, the hypothesis can be rejected at the .05 level for call options in every category except in-the-money, just out-of-the-money and at-the-money options. In addition, the hypothesis can be rejected at the .01 level for deep out-of-the-money calls. For put options, the hypothesis is rejected at the .05 for every category except deep out-of-the-money and at-the-money options. In addition, the hypothesis can be rejected at the .01 level for the complete sample, in-the-money, just in-the-money and out-of-the-money categories. It is apparent from these results that the GANN has been able to reduce pricing errors by incorporating additional economic data as neural network inputs.

Table 4.22: Paired-Comparison And Wilcoxon Test Results Of Eurodollar Futures Option GANN Approximation Methods (GANN₂ vs. GANN₁) (Panel A: Calls)

Sample Group	N	Paired t-test		Wilcoxon	
		t-statistic	p-value	Z-value	p-value
Complete Sample	6887	-2.312	0.011	-1.972	0.025
in-the-money	2698	-0.397	0.346	-0.345	0.365
just-in	1782	1.309	0.096	-1.657	0.049
deep-in	910	-2.005	0.023	-2.314	0.011
out-of-the-money	4159	-3.113	0.001	-2.088	0.019
just-out	1840	-2.391	0.008	-0.182	0.428
deep-out	2312	-1.955	0.026	-2.627	0.005
at-the-money	30	-0.235	0.408	-0.381	0.352

Table 4.22 (continued)

(Panel B: Puts)

Sample Group	N	Paired t-test		Wilcoxon	
		t-statistic	p-value	Z-value	p-value
Complete Sample	6887	-0.503	0.308	-2.534	0.006
in-the-money	4159	-1.772	0.038	-5.138	0.000
just-in	1840	-7.943	0.000	-9.812	0.000
deep-in	2312	5.107	0.000	-1.839	0.033
out-of-the-money	2698	1.412	0.079	-2.519	0.006
just-out	1782	1.018	0.155	-2.059	0.020
deep-out	910	0.976	0.165	-1.372	0.170
at-the-money	30	0.181	0.429	-0.010	0.496

The degree of moneyness is as previously described. For example, if the futures rate $(F(t))$ is greater than the strike rate (100 - K), a put option on a 3-month Eurodollar futures contract will be in-the-money and a call option will be out-of-the-money. $GANN_1$ has 4 inputs and 18 hidden layer nodes while $GANN_2$ has 6 input and 18 hidden layer nodes. All p-values represent 1-tailed test.

A final test of the GANNs developed in this study is based on their ability to generalize and handle variations in input. This is accomplished by presenting the trained GANNs with new information. Recall from the previous chapter that four additional holdout data sets were constructed (HOLDOUT2 through HOLDOUT5). HOLDOUT2 consists of all observations over the period July 1 through July 8 and contains 384 observations. HOLDOUT3 through HOLDOUT5 each have 320 observations and cover the periods July 11 through July 15, July 18 through July 22, and July 25 through July 29. Each holdout sample progressively moves farther away from the training data in time.

Table 4.23 reports the pricing errors (as measured by MAE) for the different holdout samples. The errors increase through time, confirming *a priori* expectations. Referring to Table 3.4 in the previous chapter, the distribution of the inputs for the above holdout samples appears to be significantly different from those for the training data set. Thus, it was expected that the pricing errors would be larger for the above holdout samples than they were for the HOLDOUT1 sample. The errors reported in Table 4.23 are also statistically different from zero at a .01 level of significance. It should be noted, however, that the errors produced by the $GANN_1$ and $GANN_2$ models are significantly smaller than those produced by the BS_{CS} OPM. Consequently, although the errors do increase in size through time, the GANN still provides better call and put price approximations than the BS_{CS} OPM.

The above analysis indicates the need to update the neural network connection weights on a periodic basis, as new information becomes available. This could be done on a weekly or daily basis. The ability to incorporate new information easily is, in fact, one of the advantages of neural networks. With traditional option pricing models, *a priori* assumptions about the underlying distribution of the independent variables must be made. If it turns out these assumptions are invalid, an entirely new model must be derived. With a neural network, any changes in market forces that cause the relationship between the input variables and the output variables to be altered or that change the distribution of the variables themselves, is easily captured by retraining the network to incorporate this new information.

Table 4.23: Comparison Of GANN Mean Absolute Errors For Various Holdout Samples

Holdout Sample	N	Calls			Puts	
		$GANN_1$	$GANN_2$		$GANN_1$	$GANN_2$
HOLDOUT2	384	0.02282	0.01483		0.02937	0.02459
HOLDOUT3	320	0.02736	0.01801		0.03450	0.02900
HOLDOUT4	320	0.03107	0.02607		0.03923	0.03405
HOLDOUT5	320	0.03542	0.02820		0.04141	0.03615

$GANN_1$ has 4 input nodes and 18 hidden layer nodes while $GANN_2$ has 6 input nodes and 18 hidden layer nodes.

SUMMARY

In summary, this chapter reports the application and testing of a number of neural network models developed to price interest rate futures options. First, this research examined the GANN's ability to approximate a pre-specified option pricing function through time. It was found that the GANN option price approximations were not statistically different from the simulated option prices in many of the sub-samples tested. Although the pricing errors in some sub-samples were significant, the errors were relatively small as measured by MAE. An examination of the input variables showed that the GANN arrived at logical weightings when trained on the simulated data set. Therefore, the GANN was able to accurately approximate the option pricing function used to generate the simulated call and put option prices.

Second, a number of neural networks were tested on actual market data. The results show that the GANN can indeed accurately approximate call and put option prices on the 3-month ED futures contract. Although significant pricing errors were found for just in-the-money calls, in-the-money puts, just in-the-money puts and deep in-the-money puts, the observed errors were not significant for any other category. Furthermore, although some sub-samples had significant pricing errors, the magnitudes of these errors were small. Thus, it is unlikely that a hedging strategy could be set up to take advantage of these errors that would yield profits large enough to offset transactions costs in the market.

Third, the GANN's option price approximations were compared with one of the futures options pricing models developed by Chen & Scott (1993). The neural networks significantly outperformed (in terms of MAE) the BS_{CS} OPM in every holdout sample tested. In most cases, the MAEs produced by the BS_{CS} OPM were five times larger than the MAEs produced by the GANN and in some cases, the errors were ten times larger. For the majority of the sub-samples, the average GANN error was only slightly larger than the minimum price move allowed for the option.

Next, the GANNs ability to incorporate additional economic information was tested. Neural networks were developed that had two additional input variables, one a proxy for the degree of moneyness and the other was the 3-month Eurodollar rate. These networks produced pricing errors (as measured by MAE) that were half the size of the pricing errors generated by the original networks. In fact, many of the errors were less than .01, which is the minimum tick move (price adjustment) allowed for the 3-month ED futures option. Finally, the neural networks were presented with new data to test their ability to approximate option prices when given inputs whose distribution differed from those used to train the network. As expected, the pricing errors increased as the input characteristics diverged from the original training data characteristics. Although these errors were statistically significant, the GANN consistently produced smaller errors than the BS_{CS} OPM.

NOTES

1. Here the term "moneyness" refers to the degree to which the option is in-the-money or out-of-the-money and is measured by $((100 - K) - R(t))$ for calls and $((R(t) - (100 - K)$ for puts. For example, an option that is deep in-the-money should logically have a higher value than an otherwise identical option that is at-the-money.

2. All normality plots and tests, and the Wilcoxon matched-pairs signed-rank tests were conducted using SPSS for Windows, version 6.0.

CHAPTER V

Conclusions and Suggestions for Future Research

In this chapter, the findings and results of this study are summarized. The first issue to be addressed is whether or not the goals outlined in Chapter I were achieved. Concluding remarks and implications for the investor will follow this. Finally, suggestions for further research will be discussed.

CONCLUSIONS

In Chapter I, the primary goals of this enterprise were outlined. They are summarized as follows:

1. To establish a neural network's ability to approximate a known, pre-specified, option pricing function through simulation.

2. To develop an artificial neural network that will accurately price futures options with futures-style margining using real data.

3. To examine the effects of incorporating additional economic data into the pricing of futures options when using ANNs.

As secondary objective, this study proposed to compare the ANNs ability to approximate the prices of futures options with futures-style margining with current option pricing approximation techniques. The particular model compared to was a derivation of the basic Black-

187

Scholes (1973) or Black's (1976) option pricing model developed by Chen & Scott (1993).

To address the first objective, call and put option prices were generated using a known option pricing function. From this simulated data set, a training sample consisting of 3991 observations and a holdout sample consisting of 36,412 observations were constructed. Furthermore, because Altman et al. (1994) found "illogical weightings of the indicators" in his corporate distress prediction comparison to Multiple Discriminant Analysis and Logit, a sensitivity analysis was initiated on the trained neural network connection weights.

It was shown that the genetic adaptive neural network (GANN) was able to approximate, to a high degree of accuracy, the complex, non-linear option pricing function used to produce the simulated call and put option prices. The differences in the GANN's call and put approximations were not significantly different from the simulation prices for the sample as a whole or for many of the sub-samples tested. Although the pricing errors in some sub-samples were found to be statistically significant, the errors were relatively small as measured by MAE. An examination of the input variables showed that the GANN arrived at logical weightings, thereby addressing the concerns raised by the Altman (1994) study.

To address the second objective, the GANN's ability to accurately approximate prices for the 3-month ED futures option traded on the London International Financial Futures and Options Exchange (LIFFE) was tested. Neural networks were developed that use the futures rate, the strike rate (100−the strike price), the time to maturity, and the historical volatility of the underlying futures contract as inputs. Collectively, the evidence confirms that the GANN was able to accurately approximate the real call and put values for the 3-month futures option traded on LIFFE as the pricing errors produced by the GANN were not found to be significantly different from zero in many of the sub-samples. Although significant pricing errors were found for some of the sub-samples examined, the magnitudes of the errors were small, making the prospect of a profitable hedging strategy unlikely.

The errors produced by the GANN were found to be smaller (as measured by Mean Squared Error and Mean Absolute Error) than those produced by the BS_{CS} OPM. This finding applies to the secondary objective of this study. In many cases, the MAE generated by the BS_{CS} OPM was 5 times larger than the MAE generated by the GANN. Also, the BS_{CS} OPM appears to generate pricing biases with respect to the degree of moneyness, the time to maturity, and volatility. As an additional advantage of the GANN over the BS_{CS} OPM, such spurious relationships were not found in the GANN models.

For the third objective of this study, the GANNs ability to incorporate additional economic information was tested. Neural networks were developed that included two additional input variables, a proxy for the degree of moneyness and the 3-month Eurodollar interest rate. These networks generated pricing errors (as measured by MAE) that were half the size of the pricing errors produced by the original networks. Furthermore, many of the errors were less than .01. The significance of this fact is that the minimum allowable price move for the 3-month ED futures option traded on LIFFE is .01. This means the average error generated by the GANN is less than the minimum tick move for the options being examined.

Finally, the neural networks were presented with new data to test their ability to generalize. As expected, the pricing errors increased as the input characteristics from the new data diverged from the original training data characteristics. It is important to note that under these conditions, the GANN still generated errors that were significantly smaller than the errors produced by the BS_{CS} OPM. The results of this final analysis indicate the need to update the neural network connection weights on a periodic basis as new information becomes available.

The results of this study could be of great value to an investor (either a potential writer or buyer of 3-month Eurodollar futures options). Unfortunately for the investor, there are no closed formed solutions for valuing these types of options. This requires the investor to utilize some type of approximation that is both accurate and fast. The problem is that the available approximation techniques are not very accurate for a variety of reasons. According to Hull (1993):

> Interest rate options are more difficult to value than stock options, currency options, index options, and most futures options. This is partly because we are dealing with a whole term structure—not a single variable. It is also partly because the behavior of interest rates is relatively complicated. . . . Many of the yield curve models that have been proposed have the disadvantage that they are not consistent with the term structure of interest rates at the time the model is built.

The 3-month ED option traded on LIFFE is an interest rate option. To further complicate matters, the options traded on life are traded in a manner similar to a futures contract. The buyer does not pay the premium up front, rather, he/she posts margin. This margin is typically some fraction of the premium price. Then, both the buyer and writer's accounts are marked to market on a daily basis as the value of the underlying futures contract, and hence, the value of the option changes. At the time of this writing, very few studies have addressed this type of option (Lieu [1990], Kuo [1991], Chen & Scott [1993], and Lajbcygier et al [1997]). The studies that have pertained to this issue disagree as to whether or not a risk-free rate should be included in the option pricing model. The consensus is that if both the option buyer and writer (seller) have to post equal margins, the risk-free rate should drop out.

If an investor were to utilize a neural network to approximate option prices, many of the above issues would be addressed. An investor could train his or her own network, periodically updating the weights. The connection weights could then be used to approximate call and put option prices. Although there are computation costs involved with training a network, there are no computational costs associated with evaluating the network. In fact, the connection weights and input variables could be used in conjunction with a spreadsheet to produce an instantaneous price approximation. The GANNs developed in this study meet both the investor's criteria. The approximations are both fast and accurate.

SUGGESTIONS FOR FURTHER RESEARCH

This study has shown that the genetic adaptive neural network is able to accurately approximate call and put prices for the 3-month Eurodollar futures option traded on LIFFE. It was also found to be a more accurate approximator than the BS_{CS} OPM. Three logical extensions to this research are apparent. The first is to test the GANNs performance against other approximation methods for this type of option. Chen & Scott (1993) derive two models in addition to the one compared to in this study. The models differ based on their assumptions as to interest rate behavior.

The second obvious extension would be to apply the GANN to different types of options. As mentioned in Chapter I, there are many options that have no closed form solution and therefore, must be approximated. The foreign exchange options traded on the Philadelphia Stock Exchange are a good candidate. Also, the 3-month ED futures option contract on LIFFE is thinly traded. This means that the observed prices may not accurately reflect new market information. Therefore, the GANN may be able to generate better performance by examining a heavily traded option and incorporating more economic variables as inputs.

Finally, a possible extension of this research could be to predict the future direction of price moves for a security, interest rates, security indexes and/or foreign exchange rates. Neural networks have proved successful in predicting corporate distress, the potential outcome of bankruptcy filings, and bond re-ratings. It seems likely that by using historical information one may also be able to predict the direction of a price move for some security. To date, no models have been developed that have had success in predicting future prices, interest rates or exchange rates. A model that could successfully predict in these areas, even modestly, would certainly be of great value to investors, hedgers, and policy makers.

In closing, neural networks have proven to be a valuable tool for the world of finance. They are being used to screen credit applications, spot stolen credit cards, and detect potentially fraudulent behavior. The potential applications are innumerable and research in this area should continue. With continued exponential increases in computing power, it seems likely that the utilization of artificial intelligence methods and genetic algorithms will increase likewise.

Bibliography

Altman, E., M. Giancarlo, and F. Varetto, "Corporate Distress Diagnosis: Comparisons Using Linear Discriminant Analysis and Neural Networks (the Italian experience), *Journal of Banking and Finance*, 18 (1994) 505–529.

Barone-Adesi, G., and R. Whaley, "Efficient Analytic Approximation of American Option Values," *Journal of Finance*, 1987, V42, 301–320.

Bhattacharya, M., "Empirical Properties of the Black-Sholes Formula under Ideal Conditions," Journal of Financial and Quantitative Analysis, December 1980, 1081–1106.

Biger, N., and J. Hull, "The Valuation of Currency Options," *Financial Management*, V12, (Spring 1983), 24–28.

Black, F., and M. Scholes, "The Pricing of Options and Corporate Liabilities," *Journal of Political Economy*, 1973, V83, 637–654.

Black, F., "Fact and Fantasy in the Use of Options and Corporate Liabilites," *Financial Analysts Journal*, 1975, (July–August), 36–41, 61–72.

Black, F., E. Derman, and W. Toy, "A One-factor Model of Interest Rates and its Applications to Treasury Bond Options," *Financial Analysts Journal*, 1990, (Jan–Feb) 33–39.

Bodurtha, J. N., and G. R. Courtadon, "Tests of an American Option Pricing Model on the Foreign Currency Options Market," *Journal of Financial and Quantitative Analysis*, 1987, V22, 153–167.

Brennan, M., and E. Schwartz, "The Valuation of American Put Options," *Journal of Finance*, 1977, V32, 449–462.

— — —, "Finite Difference Methods and Jump Processes Arising in the Pricing of Contingent Claims: A Synthesis," *Journal of Financial and Quantitative Analysis*, 1978, V17, 461–474.

Carverhill, A., and N. Webber, "American Options: Theory and Numerical Analysis," *Options: Recent Advances in Theory and Practice*, ed. Stewart Hodges, New York: Manchester UP, 1990, 80–94.

Chen, Ren-Raw, and Louis Scott, "Pricing Interest Rate Futures Options with Futures-Style Margining," *Journal of Futures Markets*, 1993, v13(1), 15–22.

Choi, Jin W., and Francis A. Longstaff, "Pricing Options of Agricultural Futures: An Application of the Constant Elasticity of Variance Option Pricing Model," *Journal of Futures Markets*, 1985, v5(2), 247–258.

Coats, Pamela K., and L. Franklin Fant, "Recognizing Financial Distress Patterns Using a Neural Network Tool," *Financial Management*, 1993, v22(3), 142–155.

Collins, E., S. Ghosh and C. Scofield, "An Application of a Multiple Neural Network Learning System to Emulation of Mortgage Underwriting Judgements," *Proceedings of the IEEE International Conference on Neural Networks*, 1988, 2, 459–466.

Copeland, Thomas E., and J. Fred Weston, *Financial Theory and Corporate Policy*, 3rd Ed., Addison-Wesley Publishing Company, 1988, 240–296.

Courtadon, G., "The Pricing of Options on Default-free Bonds," *Journal of Financial and Quantitative Analysis*, 17 (March 1982), pp. 75–100.

Cox, J., J. Ingersoll and S. Ross, "A theory of the Term Structure of Interest Rates," *Econometrica*, 53 (1985), 385–407.

Cox, J., and Ross, S., "The Valuation of Options for Alternative Stochastic Processes," *Journal of Financial Economics*, 3 (March 1976), 145–166.

Cox, J., Ross, S. and M. Rubenstein, "Option Pricing: A Simplified Approach," *Journal of Financial Economics*, 1979, V7, 229–263.

Davis, Kevin, "The Pricing of Options on Australian Bank Bill Futures: A Test of the Black Model Using Transactions Data," *Review of Futures Markets*, 1991, v10(3), 460–476.

Dorsey, R.E., R.O. Edmister and J.D. Johnson, "Financial Distress Prediction: A Neural Net Model for Large Corporations," Working Paper, Department of Economics and Finance, University of Mississippi, 1993.

Dorsey, R.E., J.D. Johnson and W.J. Mayer, "A Genetic Algorithm for the Training of Feedforward Neural Networks," *Advances in Artificial Intelligence in Economics, Finance, and Management*, (J.D. Johnson and A.B. Whinston, eds., 93–111), Vol. I, 1994, Greenwich, CT: JAI Press Inc.

Dorsey, R.E. and W.J. Mayer, "Genetic Algorithms for Estimation Problems with Multiple Optima, Non-Differentiability, and Other Irregular

Features," *Journal of Business and Economic Statistics*, Vol. 13, No. 1, 53–66.

————, "Optimization Using Genetic Algorithms," *Advances in Artificial Intelligence in Economics, Finance, and Management*, (J.D. Johnson and A.B. Whinston, eds.), Vol. I, Greenwich, CT: JAI Press Inc., 69–91.

Dutta, S., and S. Shekhar, "Bond Rating: A Non-conservative Application of Neural Networks," *Proceedings of the IEEE International Conference on Neural Networks*, 2 1988, 443–450.

Eytan, T. Hanan, and Giora Harpaz, "The Pricing of Futures and Options Contracts on the Value Line Index," *Journal of Finance*, 1986, v41(4), 843–856.

Galai, D., "Tests of Market Efficiency of the Chicago Board of Options Exchange," *Journal of Business*, April 1977, 167–197.

Garman, M. B., and S. W. Kohlhagen, "Foreign Currency Option Values," *Journal of International Money and Finance*, 1983, v2, 231–237.

Gay, Gerald D., and Steven Manaster, "Equilibrium Treasury Bond Futures Pricing in the Presence of Implicit Delivery Options," *Journal of Futures Markets*, 1991, v11(5), 623–646.

Geske, R., "The Valuation of Compound Options," *Journal of Financial Economics*, 7 (1979), 63–81.

Geske, R., and H. Johnson, "The American Put Valued Analytically," *Journal of Finance*, 1984, V39, 1511–1524.

Geske, R., and R. Roll, "On Valuing American Call Options with the Black-Scholes Formula," *Journal of Finance*, 1984, 39, 443–455.

Gibson, R., and E.S. Schwartz, "The Pricing of Crude Oil Futures Options Contracts," *Advances in Futures and Options Research*, 1993, v6, 291–311.

Grabbe, J. O., "The Pricing of Call and Put Options on Foreign Exchange," *Journal of International Money and Finance*, 1983, V2, 239–253.

Grundnitski, Gary, and Larry Osburn, "Forecasting S&P and Gold Futures Prices: An Application of Neural Networks," *Journal of Futures Markets*, 1993, v13(6), 631–643.

Hatfield, Gay B., and A. Jay White, "Bond Rating Changes: Neural Net Estimates for Bank Holding Companies," 1998, Working Paper.

Hauser, Robert J., and David Neff, "Pricing Options on Agricultural Futures: Departures from Traditional Theory," *Journal of Futures Markets*, 1985, v5(4), 539–577.

Hawley, Delvin D., John D. Johnson and Dijjotam Raina, "Artificial Neural Systems: A New Tool for Financial Decision-Making," *Financial Analyst Journal*, 1990, v46(6), 63–72.

Hilliard, J.E., J. Madura and A.L. Tucker, "Currency Option Pricing with Stochastic Domestic and Foreign Interest Rates," *Journal of Financial and Quantitative Analysis*, 1991, 26 (2), 139–151.

Ho, T.S.Y., and S.B. Lee, "Term Structure Movements and Pricing Interest Rate Contingent Claims," *Journal of Finance*, 1986, 41, 1011–1029.

Hofmann, N., E. Platen and M. Schweizer, "Option Pricing Under Incompleteness and Stochastic Volatility," *Mathematical Finance*, 1992, 2 (3), 153–187.

Hornik, K., M. Stinchcombe and H. White, "Multilayer Feedforward Networks are Universal Approximators," *Technical Report 88-45R*, 1989, University of California at San Diego.

— — —, "Universal Approximation of an Unknown Mapping and its Derivatives Using Multilayer Feedforward Networks," *Technical Report 89-36R*, 1990, University of California at San Diego.

Hull, John, *Options, Futures, and Other Derivative Securities*, 2nd Ed., Prentice-Hall, 1993, 190–244, 329–411, and 434–452.

Hull, J. C., and Alan White, "The Pricing of Options on Assets with Stochastic Volatilities," *Journal of Finance*, 42 (June 1987), 281–300.

— — —, "An Analysis of the Bias in Option Pricing Caused by Stochastic Volatility," *Advances in Futures and Options Research*, 3 (1988) 27–61.

— — —, "Pricing Interest Rate Derivative Securities,"*Review of Financial Studies*, 1990, 3(4), 573–92.

Hutchinson, James, Andrew Lo, and Tomaso Poggio, "A Nonparametric Approach to Pricing and Hedging Derivative Securities Via Learning Networks," *Journal of Finance*, v49(3), July 1984, pp. 851–890.

Jamshidian, F., "An Exact Bond Option Pricing Formula," *Journal of Finance*, 44 (March 1989), 205–219.

Keen, John, "Genetic Algorithms for Market Trading," *AI in Finance*, Winter 1995, 25–39.

Kolb, Robert W., *Futures, Options, and Swaps*, Kolb Publishing Company, 1994, 485–641.

Kolmogorov, A. N., "On the Representation of Continuous Function of Many Variables by Superposition of Continuous Functions of One Variable and Addition," *American Mathematical Society Translation*, 28, 1963, pp. 55–59.

Kryzanowski, Lawrence, Michael Galler and David W. Wright, "Using Artificial Neural Networks to Pick Stocks," *Financial Analyst Journal*, 1993, v49(4), 21–27.

Lajbcygier, Paul, Andrew Flitman, Anthony Swan, and Rob Hyndman, "The Pricing and Trading of Options Using a Hybrid Neural Network Model with Historical Volatility," *NeuroVest Journal*, v5,(1), January/February 1997, pp. 27–40.

Lee, Sang Bin, and Sung Moo Huh, "Futures Market Timing Ability With Neural Networks," *Review of Futures Markets*, 1991, v10(3), 534–547.

Lieu, Derming. "Option Pricing With Futures-Style Margining," *Journal of Futures Markets*, 1990, v10(4), 327–338.

MacBeth, J., and L. Merville, "An Empirical Examination of the Black-Sholes Call Option Pricing Model," *Journal of Finance*, December 1979, 1173–1186.

– – –, "Tests of the Black-Scholes and Cox Call Option Valuation Models," *Journal of Finance*, May 1980, 285–300.

MacMillan, L. "Analytical Approximation for the American Put Option," *Advances in Futures and Options Research*," V1, 119–139.

McLeod, Robert W., D. K. Malhotra and Rashmi Malhotra, "Predicting Credit Risk: A Neural Network Approach," *Journal of Retail Banking*, 1993, v15(3), 37–40.

Medsker, Larry, Efraim Turban and Robert R. Trippi, "Neural Network Fundamentals For Financial Analysts," *Journal of Investing*, 1993, v1(3), 59–68.

Melino, A., and S. Turnbull, "Pricing Foreign Currency Options with Stochastic Volatility," *Journal of Econometrics*, 1990, 45, 239–265.

Merton, R. C., "Theory of Rational Option Pricing," *Bell Journal of Economics and Management Science*, 4(Spring 1973), 141–183.

– – –, "Option Pricing When Underlying Stock Returns are Discontinuous," *Journal of Financial Economics*, 3 (March 1976), 125–144.

Pan, Zuohong, Xiaodi Liu, and Olugbenga Mejabi, "A Neural-Fuzzy System for Financial Forecasting," *Neurovest Journal*, v5(1), January/February 1997, 7–15.

Park, Hun Y. and R. Stephen Sears, "Changing Volatility and the Pricing of Options on Stock Index Futures," *Journal of Financial Research*, 1985, v8(4), 265–274.

Randolph, William L., "The Relative Pricing of Options on Futures and Options on the Spot," *Review of Futures Markets*, 1986, v5(3), 198–215.

Rendleman, R., Jr., and B. Bartter, "Two-State Option Pricing," *Journal of Finance*, December 1979, 1093–1110.

— — —, "The Pricing of Options on Debt Securities," *Journal of Financial and Quantitative Analysis*, March 1980, 11–24.

Roll, R., "An Analytic Valuation Formula for Unprotected American Call Options on Stocks with Known Dividends," *Journal of Financial Economics*, November 1977, 251–258.

Ross, S., "Options and Efficiency," *Quarterly Journal of Economics*, February 1976, 75–89.

Rubinstein, M., "The Valuation of Uncertain Income Streams and the Pricing of Options," *Bell Journal of Economics*, Autumn 1976, 407–426.

— — —, "Displaced Diffusion Option Pricing," *Journal of Finance*, March 1983, 213–265.

— — —, "Nonparametric Tests of Alternative Option Pricing Models," *Journal of Finance*, June 1985, 455–480.

Rumelhart, D. E., G.G. Hinton and R. J. Williams, "Learning Internal Representations by Error Propagation", *Parallel Distributed Processing: Exploration in the Microstructure of Cognition*, Vol. I, D.E. Rumelhart and J.L. McClelland (Eds.), MIT Press: Mass., 1986, 318–62.

Salchenberger, L. M., E. M. Cinar and N. A. Lash, "Neural Networks: A New Tool for Predicting Thrift Failures," *Decision Sciences*, 23, 1992, 899–916.

Sexton, R., J. Johnson and R. Dorsey, "Obtaining a Global Optimum for Neural Networks," Working Paper, Department of Economics and Finance, University of Mississippi, 1995.

Shandle, J., "Neural Networks are Ready for Prime Time," *Electronic Design*, February 18, 1993, 51–58.

Shastri, Kuldeep and Kishore Tandon, "Options on Futures Contracts: A comparison of European and American Pricing Models," *Journal of Futures Markets*, 1986a, v6(4), 593–618.

— — —, "An Empirical Test of a Valuation Model for American Options on Futures Contracts." *Journal of Financial & Quantitative Analysis*, 1986b, v21(4), 377–392.

Smith, C., "Option Pricing Review," *Journal of Financial Economics*, January–March 1976, 1–51.

— — —, *The Modern Theory of Corporate Finance*, 2nd Ed., North-Holland Publishing Company, 1990, 345–387.

Trippi, Robert R., and Duane Desieno, "Trading Equity Index Futures With a Neural Network," *Journal of Portfolio Management*, 1992, v19(1), 27–33.

Vasicek, O., "An Equilibrium Characterization of the Term Structure," *Journal of Financial Economics*, 5 (1977), 177–88.

Whaley, R., "On the Valuation of American Call Options on Stocks with Known Dividends," *Journal of Financial Economics*, 9 (June 1981), 207–211.

— — —, "Valuation of American Call Options on Dividend Paying Stocks: Empirical Tests," *Journal of Financial Economics*, 1982, 29–58.

— — —, "Valuation of American Futures Options: Theory and Empirical Tests," *Journal of Financial Economics*, 16 (March 1986), 127–150.

White, A. Jay, "A Genetic Adaptive Neural Network Approach to Pricing Options: A Simulation Analysis," *Journal of Computational Intelligence in Finance*, v6(2), March/April 1998, pp. 13–23.

White, A. Jay, G. Hatfield, and R. Dorsey, "A Genetic Adaptive Neural Network Approach to Pricing Options With Futures Style Margining," Working Paper, 1998.

Wolf, Avner, "Options of Futures: Pricing and the Effect of an Anticipated Price Change," *Journal of Futures Markets*, 1984, v4 (4), 491–512.

Yao, Jingtao, Yili Li, and Chew Lim Tan, "Forecasting the CHF-USD Exchange Rates using Neural Networks," *Journal of Computational Intelligence in Finance*, v5(2), March/April 1997, 7–13.

Author Index

A
Altman, E. I., 102, 143, 188

B
Barone-Adesi, G., 33
Bartter, B., 24
Bhattacharya, M., 17
Black, F., 5, 9–17, 17–19, 42–44,
    188
Bower, 102
Brennan, M.J., 37

C
Chance, 16, 68, 89
Chen, R., 54, 65, 115, 190
Cinar, E.M., 102, 113
Coats, P.K., 102
Collins, E., 102
Copeland, T.E., 31, 63
Cox, J.C., 21, 24, 49, 59

D
Dorsey, R.E., 110, 163
Dutta, S., 102

F
Fant, L.F., 102

G
Gailai, D., 17
Garman, M.B., 44
Geske, R., 22–24, 60
Ghosh, S., 102

H
Hatfield, G.B., 102, 163
Ho, T.S.Y., 50
Hornik, K., 111
Hull, J., 6, 21, 50, 61, 63, 189
Hutchinson, J. 102

I
Ingersoll, J.E., 21, 49

J
Johnson, J.D., 6, 110

K
Kean J., 110
Kolb, R.W., 41
Kohlhagen, S.W., 44

201

Subject Index